THE UNEMPLOYED MAN AND HIS FAMILY

CLASSICS IN GENDER STUDIES

Series Editor Michael S. Kimmel
Dept. of Sociology, SUNY at Stony Brook

Each generation of scholars rediscovers the "classics" that it needs. These works ground our contemporary research and provide historical context. What makes them "classics" is not simply that they're old, but that they continue to speak to contemporary concerns. Sadly, many brilliant works by major scholars and thinkers that were so influential in their time have passed out of print. The books in this series will reintroduce these works both to established scholars and to a new generation of students and researchers as they examine the origins of our understanding of contemporary gender relations.

BOOKS IN THE SERIES

The Home: Its Work and Influence, Charlotte Perkins Gilman (2002)
Reprint of the 1903 edition with an introduction by Michael S. Kimmel

Concerning Children, Charlotte Perkins Gilman (2003)
Reprint of the 1900 edition with an introduction by Michael S. Kimmel

His Religion and Hers: A Study of the Faith of Our Fathers and the Work of Our Mothers, Charlotte Perkins Gilman (2003)
Reprint of the 1923 edition with an introduction by Michael S. Kimmel

Fat and Blood; And How to Make Them, S. Weir Mitchell (2004)
Reprint of the 1882 edition with an introduction by Michael S. Kimmel

Wear and Tear; Or, Hints for the Overworked, S. Weir Mitchell (2004)
Reprint of the 1973 Arno Press reprint edition, introduction by Michael S. Kimmel

Women in the Modern World: Their Education and Their Dilemmas, Mirra Komarovsky (2004), Reprint of the 1953 edition with an introduction by Michael S. Kimmel

Dilemmas of Masculinity: A Study of College Youth, Mirra Komarovsky (2004)
Reprint of the 1976 edition with an introduction by Michael S. Kimmel

Women in College: Shaping New Feminine Identities, Mirra Komarovsky (2004)
Reprint of the 1985 edition with an introduction by Michael S. Kimmel

The Unemployed Man and His Family: The Effect of Unemployment upon the Status of the Man in Fifty-Nine Families, Mirra Komarovsky (2004)
Reprint of the 1971 Octagon Books edition with an introduction by Michael S. Kimmel

ABOUT THE SERIES EDITOR

Michael S. Kimmel is professor of sociology at the State University of New York, Stony Brook. His publications include *The Politics of Manhood* (1996), *Manhood in America: A Cultural History* (1996), and *The Gendered Society* (2000). He is the current editor of the international, interdisciplinary journal *Men and Masculinities*.

Classics in Gender Studies Series
AltaMira Press, 1630 North Main Street #367, Walnut Creek, CA 94596
(925) 938-7243, www.altamirapress.com

THE UNEMPLOYED MAN AND HIS FAMILY

THE EFFECT OF UNEMPLOYMENT UPON THE STATUS OF THE MAN IN FIFTY-NINE FAMILIES

MIRRA KOMAROVSKY

INTRODUCED BY
MICHAEL S. KIMMEL

ALTAMIRA
PRESS

A Division of
ROWMAN & LITTLEFIELD PUBLISHERS, INC.
Walnut Creek • Lanham • New York • Toronto • Oxford

ALTAMIRA PRESS
A division of Rowman & Littlefield Publishers, Inc.
1630 North Main Street, #367
Walnut Creek, CA 94596
www.altamirapress.com

Rowman & Littlefield Publishers, Inc.
A wholly owned subsidiary of The Rowman & Littlefield Publishing Group, Inc.
4501 Forbes Boulevard, Suite 200
Lanham, MD 20706

PO Box 317
Oxford
OX2 9RU, UK

British Library Cataloguing in Publication Information Available

Library of Congress Catalog Car No. 73-120637

ISBN 0-7591-0731-9 (alk. paper)—ISBN 0-7591-0732-7 (pbk.: alk. paper)

Printed in the United States of America
♾™ The paper used in this publication meets the minimum requirements of American
National Standard for Information Sciences—Permanence of Paper for Printed Library
Materials, ANSI/NISO Z39.48–1992.

CONTENTS

PREFACE

IN the struggle between the systems of social philosophy the question of the relative importance of the separate realms of culture is one of the most fundamental for the historical process. While one side hails the ideal, religious, moral, or national factors as decisive, others claim that the economic factors are the determining ones. To clarify such questions it is not sufficient to introduce considerations of a general character or to collect facts intended to support one thesis or the other. We are much more in need of series of research studies which disclose the interrelation of the various forces in specific social institutions. One of the institutions in which the interrelationship may profitably be studied is the family.

In 1931 the International Institute of Social Research undertook studies of the family in contemporary society. The first results were published in 1936 in a voluminous symposium on Authority and the Family (Librairie Félix Alcan, Paris, 1936). Dr. Komarovsky's book represents a continuation of the earlier studies, which were largely concerned with European countries. It reports on an investigation undertaken by the Institute in the Winter of 1935-1936, after its transfer to New York.

While the number of cases studied was small, the publication of the study may be of some use for those who, like ourselves, have to struggle with the methodological difficulties which beset empirical investigations of the interrelationship of the separate cultural factors.

The study was conducted by Dr. Mirra Komarovsky with the collaboration of Dr. Paul F. Lazarsfeld.

We are indebted to Professors Robert S. Lynd, Robert M. MacIver, Willard W. Waller, and Louis Wirth for reading the manuscript and offering valuable criticisms.

We wish to acknowledge, also, the assistance given by Mrs. Hazel Gaudet, Mr. Samuel Geller, and Dr. Richard Ohmes in the collection of the material, and by Miss Eunice Goddard in the preparation of the manuscript.

MAX HORKHEIMER
Director, Institute of Social Research

COLUMBIA UNIVERSITY IN
THE CITY OF NEW YORK
June, 1940

SERIES EDITOR'S INTRODUCTION
Michael S. Kimmel

I CAME to know Mirra Komarovsky only toward the end of her life. In 1990, I was invited to give a talk at the Barnard Women's Center about the documentary history I was working on about men's support of feminism. Seated quietly in the back of the packed room was this well-dressed, elegant, elderly woman, whom I did not recognize. At the end of my talk, she came up to me and introduced herself. My jaw must have dropped; I wasn't used to having eminent professors come to the lectures of a then lowly assistant professor.

She was both warm and sympathetic, and gave me some very sage advice about how to think about men who had supported women's equality. I sent her a copy of the book when it came out, and she and I exchanged letters briefly after that. Then she invited me to tea—or rather, I suppose, it's more accurate to say I was "summoned." I received an invitation, by mail, to come for tea on a weekday afternoon. We sat in her parlor of her Upper West Side apartment for more than two hours, talking about the special "dilemmas of masculinity" as we watched the sun gradually set over the Hudson River.

What struck me in that brief meeting was her compassion for the predicaments that men were facing in negotiating a sex-role system in which they are also, of course, privileged. Men had a tough time juggling incompatible role demands and would often feel quite off-kilter. This compassion about these contradictions in gender relations was the centerpiece for all her work.

Komarovsky was among the most creative role theorists to emerge from a generation of colleagues and students of the Columbia School of Sociology—influenced by Robert Merton, William J. Goode, and others. Unlike other role theorists, though, Komarovsky focused on conflict, especially because social change had transformed roles only partially. It was in the seams of those changes, the cracks in the older edifices, that she saw the current anguish of many women (and later, of men) and also observed the potential for change. She devoted her ASA Presidential address to this topic and wrote on it for more than thirty years.

Unlike Parsons, who saw the division of the family into expres-

ix

sive and instrumental roles as functional, Komarovsky saw this division as creating terrible conflicts for women, as they struggled to claim their ambitions and aspirations, and later for men, as they struggled to accept the enormous changes that had taken place among women.

Komarovsky will no doubt be remembered for her pioneering study of the contradictions in women's lives. In two of her most important books, *Women in the Modern World* (1953) and *Women in College* (1985) she showed how contradictory were the demands on women—that they perform well in school and that they downplay their intellectual abilities to land a man. But from her earliest work, she was also interested in how internally inconsistent and contradictory were these gender expectations for men.

In fact, with the exception of *Blue Collar Marriage*, her most famous book, Komarovsky's career vacillates between the study of men and the study of women. After her PhD thesis, she turned her attention to women for her 1953 book. But then, after the enormous success of *Blue Collar Marriage*, she returned to men in 1976 in *Dilemmas of Masculinity*, only to return to women again in 1985 in *Women in College*. And throughout she listened carefully to both the women and the men with whom she spoke, and she heard their pain of trying to live up to impossible standards, of trying to reconcile their ambitions with the expectations of society.

This is evident in her earliest book, her poignant work on masculinity in the Great Depression, *The Unemployed Man and His Family* (1940), which described how the loss of breadwinner status eroded moral authority of father at home. The unemployed man, she wrote, "suffers from deep humiliation" since he fails in his core role as family provider. He appears bewildered, "as if the ground has gone out from under his feet."[1]

Many of the men she interviewed described the "humiliation within the family" as the "hardest part" of being unemployed. With their economic power eliminated, their status as head of the household was eroded and with it their sense of manhood. "When a man is at home all day he cannot possibly command as much respect as when he returns to the family for a few hours of concentrated conversation," noted one of her interview subjects. He felt himself to be a "fallen idol" without a job.[2]

"Before the Depression," said another, "I wore the pants in this family and rightly so. During the Depression I lost something.

---

[1] Mirra Komarovsky, *The Unemployed Man and His Family* (New York: Dryden, 1940), p. 74–5.

[2] Ibid., p. 355.

Maybe you call it self-respect, but in losing it I also lost the respect of my children, and I am afraid I am losing my wife."[3]

Not only was *The Unemployed Man* a substantively interesting work, but it also revealed a methodological sensitivity that was rarely, if ever, seen in sociology. In one review, R. C. Angell (past president of the ASA) called it "the greatest step forward in the personal document method since *The Polish Peasant*."[4] One is almost tempted to attribute her remarkable methodological success to her gender—an attribution with which she would no doubt have been terribly uncomfortable.

From that early study, Mirra went on to contribute significantly to our understanding of women's experiences. In *Blue Collar Marriage* (1964), she explored the intersection of class and gender, and revealed the ways that following traditional gender norms led to enormous strain in the lives of working class men and women. And, nearly forty years later following *The Unemployed Man*, in 1976, she returned to this inquiry in *Dilemmas of Masculinity*. Here she pointed out the contradictions between the "modern" ideal that a man should have intellectual companionship with dating partners and the more traditional ideas of male intellectual superiority that then leads to intellectual rivalry. She wrote in an article in anticipation of the book that the "traditional norm of male intellectual superiority conflicts with a newer norm of intellectual companionship between the sexes."[5]

Conformity to traditional norms of masculinity also led to significant strain for men after college. For example, being a secure breadwinner depends on large-scale economic processes, as well as race, education, age, and so on. Some men therefore experience what Komarovsky called a "socially structured scarcity of resources."

She also noted another source of strain for men in failing to live up to traditional norms. In her 1973 ASA Presidential Address, she found that nearly half (45 percent) of elite male undergraduates exhibited, as she wrote, "mild to acute anxiety over their failure in relationships with women, to live up to the traditional ideal of superior masculine assertiveness, determination, decisiveness, courage, independence, aggressiveness, and stability in the face of stress."[6]

Komarovsky was able to document this strain because she did

[3] Ibid., p. 357.

[4] Cited in Shulamit Reinharz, "Finding a Sociological Voice: The Work of Mirra Komarovsky" in *Sociological Inquiry* 59(4), November, 1989, p. 389.

[5] Mirra Komarovsky, "Cultural Contradictions and Sex Roles: The Masculine Case" in *American Journal of Sociology*, 78(4), 1973, p. 873.

[6] Mirra Komarovsky, "Presidential Address: Some Problems in Role Analysis" in *American Sociological Review*, 38(6), 1973, p. 655.

something rare in social science research—she listened compassionately to men's voices. That's often been very difficult for feminist researchers—to carefully listen to the men when they speak of pain and suffering. After all, men have all the privilege, all the power in our society. Whatever do they have to complain about?

Komorovsky actually explained what men have to complain about, without for a moment under-estimating the enormous privileges that accrue to men because of their gender. Hers was engaged proto-feminist scholarship that cared deeply about both the men and the women she interviewed, and who believed that the "socially structured" organization of gender relations took an enormous psychological and sociological toll on both women and men.

II.

Komarovsky was born in 1905 in Baku, a city in the Caucasus, to Jewish professional parents. In 1922, at the age of 17, her family emigrated to the United States. Shortly after they settled in Wichita, Kansas, Mirra moved to New York City, and began her lifelong association with Barnard College. She graduated from Barnard in 1926 and immediately enrolled in graduate school across the street at Columbia, where she earned her MA in 1927. She worked closely with William F. Ogburn, who supervised her MA thesis.

Ogburn was her first serious mentor, but he was discouraging when she informed him that she intended to pursue a career in sociology. "Not a realistic plan," he told her. "You are a woman, foreign born, and Jewish. I would recommend some other occupation." When Ogburn left Columbia, Komarovsky was uncertain about her future, and sought a teaching position outside the city.[7]

After brief stays at Skidmore College, where she was an instructor, and Yale, where she was a research assistant to Dorothy Thomas, she returned to New York for the remainder of her life. She became a naturalized citizen in 1930 and began to work towards her PhD at Columbia. She worked with George Lundberg, Robert MacIver and eventually wrote her dissertation under the supervision of Paul Lazersfeld. This dissertation, "The Unemployed Man and His Family," was formally submitted in 1940, and published by Dryden Press that same year.

She began teaching at Barnard in 1934, and by the time she finished her PhD, she was a full-time member of the department. Both

---

[7] See Rosalind Rosenberg, "Mirra Komarovsky" at www.columbia.edu/~rr91/ 3567/sample_biographies/mirra_komarovsky (accessed September 23, 2003).

personally and professionally, she was captivated by the cultural contradictions that defined and constrained women's lives. Along with several other women from the first generation of women PhDs (including Jessie Bernard), she became fascinated by the ways in which women of ambition and promise were both personally and institutionally thwarted in realizing their ambitions. Her field of "Marriage and the Family" was more or less the "ladies auxiliary" of sociology, and considered suitable for females, but not "real" sociology.

After World War II, two events marked her emergence onto a larger sociological stage. Millicent McIntosh assumed the presidency of Barnard in 1947 and recognized Komarovsky's talents, and, at the same time, she married a man, Marcus Heyman, who respected her intellect and supported her career ambitions. As Shulamit Reinharz writes, she and her husband "established a rewarding, egalitarian relationship which became one implicit model for her analysis of women's lives."[8]

Established, with professional confidence, institutional support and personal contentment, Komarovsky embarked on her prolific career. In 1946, Komarovsky published a landmark article in *American Journal of Sociology* on "The Cultural Contradictions of Sex Roles." Here, she anticipated the arguments of Betty Friedan and other feminists—by two decades! With Margaret Mead, Komarovsky was, Reinharz observes, "the first sociologist of the twentieth century to define women's status as a social problem."[9]

Komarovsky found that the roles imposed on college-age women after World War II were "incompatible," culturally contradictory. Gifted, ambitious women ended up "playing dumb," she argued, because it was impossible to "own" their ambitions and abilities and still maintain a social life with male students. This pivotal article was a mainstay in sociology courses for decades, and provided the basis for her book *Women in the Modern World* (1953). Perhaps her most famous book was *Blue Collar Marriage* (1967).

When she retired from the Barnard faculty in 1970, at the mandatory retirement age of 65, she continued her career within the professional associations and also as a researcher and publisher. Over the course of her life, she served her profession in many ca-

---

[8] Shulamit Reinharz, "Finding a Sociological Voice," p. 380. I have relied extensively on this essay and also Shulamt Reinharz, "Mirra Komarovsky" in *Women in Sociology: A Bio-Bibliographical Sourcebook*, Mary Jo Deegan, ed. (New York: Greenwood Press, 1991). I am grateful to Shulamit Reinharz for sharing her work with me.

[9] Mirra Komarovsky, "Cultural Contradictions and Sex Roles" in *American Journal of Socioogy*, 78(1), 1946; see Shulamit Reinharz, "Finding a Sociological Voice", p. 382.

pacities—as the Vice President (1949) and President (1955) of the
Eastern Sociological Society, Associate Editor of the *American Sociological Review* and, eventually, President of the American Sociological Association (1972).

As Shulamit Reinarz argues, Komarovsky "provided an intellectual link between the first generation of American female sociolo-
gists"—such as Jane Addams, Charlotte Perkins Gilman, Elsie
Clews Parsons—who emerged at the tail end of the first great wave
of feminism at the turn of the twentieth century, and the next
group. That second group of leaders were part of what became
known as the second wave of feminism beginning in the first few
years of the 1960s, following on the heels of Betty Friedan's *The
Feminine Mystique* (1963), a book Komarovsky's own work anticipated by a decade.[10]

A fiercely private person, she devoted her professional life to ad-
vancing women's status, especially within higher education. When
asked by her friend and colleague Cynthia Fuchs Epstein in 1989
about her then fifty-year career about women's progress, Komarovsky answered "It's been a harder job than we thought we'd have.
Who reads our work? Other women. We're ghettoized." Epstein
asked what, then, is to be done? As Epstein reports, "[h]er eyes
flashed, as was typical of this passionate and determined woman.
Without equivocation she answered 'push.'"[11]

Hers is a rich legacy, a body of work animated by a constant pas-
sion for equality and a sense that through education, social change
might indeed be possible. "We need," she wrote in 1976, "to present to both men and women more vivid models of egalitarian relationships between the sexes in order to replace the traditional ones
so deeply etched in social consciousness."[12]

Mirra Komarovsky died on January 30, 1999.[13]

III.

In *The Unemployed Man and His Family*, Komarovsky poses the
question: "what happens to the authority of the male head of the
family when he fails as a provider?" (p. 1). Between 1935 and 1936,
she interviewed 59 families in which the male had been unem-

[10] Reinharz, p. 391.
[11] Cynthia Fuchs Epstein, in "Colleagues Remember Mirra Komarovsky" in
Footnotes, May-June, 1999, p. 4.
[12] Mirra Komarovsky, *Dilemmas of Masculinity*, p. 249.
[13] This was, ironically, the day my son was born, a day I began to more experi-
entially understand the "dilemmas of masculinity" and the lag between changing desires and persistent role definitions.

ployed for at least a year. All were white, native born, Protestant, working and middle class, with at least one child over age 10. All had been in "traditional" roles—that is to say the husband had been the sole provider prior to his unemployment.

Of these, 44 reported little or no change in the father's status, while 13 reported a loss of status (p. 23). In many cases, the husband's defeat in the economic sphere did not offset the solidity and happiness of the marital relationship (p. 55). "Money isn't everything," observed one wife. "When you get a husband who is as good to you as my husband is to me, you can certainly consider yourself lucky." Another echoed this. "My husband is not a millionaire, but he is a good husband and a good father" (p. 56).

To be sure, a few of the women complained. "When a husband cannot provide to the family and makes you worry so, you lose your love for him," commented one woman. And another said, "Of course I hate my husband for bringing hardships upon the family" (p. 49).

But unemployment seems to have affected the men's sense of their own position more than it did their wives' estimation of their husbands. For one thing, it undermined their sense of themselves as breadwinners. Most found it unbearably humiliating to accept relief (p. 116).

Perhaps her most important finding was that those men who thought of themselves exclusively as provider suffered far more than those who had developed alternative identities as father and husband. It turned out that even in the throes of the Depression, maintaining a balance between work and family roles was good for men's health.

And it influenced their experience with their children. "Now that I am at home all day, I get irritated with the children and they feel that I have become a nag. When I used to work I would ask my wife in the evening 'Were Johnnie and Willie good boys today?' and then I would either punish or reward them. And that's how it should be" (p. 84).

Unemployment actually dramatically affected men's relationships with other men—perhaps even more drastically than it did with their wives. Losing their job led to a rapid and near-complete attenuation of their social life; virtually all the unemployed men reported that they had virtually no social life whatever (p. 122).

And it even affected their sex lives. Of the 38 cases in which there was sufficient information to code, 16 reported no change (42 percent), while 22 (58 percent) reported that sexual activity declined, and 4 of them reported that it had ceased altogether (p. 130).

In the end, unemployment makes a man feel like less of a man.

SERIES EDITOR'S INTRODUCTION

"It is awful to be old and discarded at 40," commented one man. "A man is not a man without work" (p. 133).

IV.

From her earliest work, Komarovsky remained optimistic about the possibilities of change. As early as 1953, she discerned "the norms emerging on and off university campuses to see the outlines of a happier alternative. We encounter young people for whom the old stereotypes have lost much of their meaning."[14] She argues strenuously for a transformation of both women's and men's roles. If, she writes in *Women in the Modern World*, "we cannot give men their former advantages, the best chance of adjustment would come through less rigid definition of masculine and feminine roles and a wider range of accepted patterns of life."[15]

In all, Komarovky believed that a *good society* "includes the acceptance of symmetrical role allocation in marriage, with both partners sharing in work, child rearing, and homemaking, making use of whatever innovations may develop to relieve the individual family of full responsibility for housekeeping chores which certainly could be performed more efficiently than they are at present." This would "release the creative potential of the female half of its citizens an provide a less constricted range of choices for the males to lead lives congenial to their capacities and inclinations."[16]

As she wrote in an op-ed article in the *New York Times* in 1981:

> Young women are becoming aware that the call to equal opportunities for women outside the home is an empty slogan as long as the society insists on traditional role segregation within the family. Some women react to this discovery with equanimity, others with frustration, resignation or indignation. But the real touchstone of their aspirations is the longing for a society in which the rhetoric of equality will be realized as fact. There is no denying that this would require major institutional changes.[17]

As early as 1953, Komarovsky concluded her study of women in the modern world by arguing that while it is "uncertain whether nature or motherhood have really made the feminine sex, in general, more kindly, humane, understanding, sympathetic, and coop-

[14] Mirra Komarovsky, *Women in the Modern World* (New York: Little Brown, 1953), p. 85.
[15] *Ibid.*, p. 300.
[16] *Dilemmas.*, p. 254, 256.
[17] Cited in http://www.undelete.org/woa/woa08–07.html (accessed September 23, 2003).

erative" the appeal to those traits for women "will begin to bear fruit only when men, too, accept that challenge and, together with women, carry on the task of making a better world." Thirty years later, the majority of the women in the 1980s she interviewed "dreamed of a society in which the father's role in child rearing is given its due importance. They envisioned a world in which the demands of work and family life are balanced by institutional reorganization and social innovations—a world with more symmetrical and egalitarian gender roles."[18]

A dream as yet unfulfilled. Yet the sociological research of Mirra Komarovsky remains among the most important expressions of the yearnings of American women for lives that are as fulfilling emotionally as they are professionally.

ABOUT THE SERIES EDITOR

MICHAEL S. KIMMEL is professor of sociology at the State University of New York at Stony Brook. His publications include *The Politics of Manhood* (1996), *Manhood in America: A Cultural History* (1996), and *The Gendered Society* (2000). He is the current editor of the international, interdisciplinary journal *Men and Masculinities*.

[18] *Women in the Modern World*, p. 300; *Women in College*, p. 319.

INTRODUCTION

THE progress of social research depends from a methodological point of view upon two factors: our ability to develop tools for quantitative measurement, and an increasing understanding of those research operations which usually are called qualitative. The present study did not offer an opportunity for refined quantitative methods, but it endeavored to contribute a more careful analysis of those nonquantitative procedures which very often are left to the haziness of "common sense." An assumption is often made that only quantitative procedures can be communicated, whereas all other procedures (insight, understanding) must be left to the inspiration of the student and to the exigencies of the problem at hand. The nonquantitative methods cannot be formulated as explicitly as an arithmetic computation. But these procedures, now clothed in ambiguous terms, still remain to be described and standardized.

This introduction serves to draw the attention of the reader to those passages in the report which deal with the psychological and logical structure of these nonquantitative operations involved in the collection and the analysis of the cases. The instructions to the interviewers (see pages 15-21) aimed to give the case studies a maximum of concreteness. The preliminary outline for the interview was drawn up on the basis of all the knowledge of family life which the investigator possessed. An attempt was made to anticipate situations which, in this particular group of families, would reveal changes in authority relations and to devise tests for these changes. The direct and general questions on attitudes were asked only after the indirect manifestations of changes had been elicited. During the interview the investigators attempted to follow the course of the respondent's own experiences in order to avoid "memory pockets." But the keynote of the instructions to the interviewers was the insistence upon concreteness. No general testimony was to be accepted without understanding its meaning in terms of concrete experience. If a man stated that his wife "respected him less" than previously, he was asked how he recognized this change; if a man was called "cranky" by another member of the family, the particular occasions in which this "crankiness" showed up were ferreted out.*

With the help of this type of case study it was possible to apply to the analysis what this text calls the technique of "discerning," described in detail on pages 135-146. The main methodological contribution of this study lies in its description of an effort to isolate the causes of a single event. Innumerable are the discussions of what "interpretation" means—whether it is a legitimate procedure in the social sciences, and how it is related to the notion of scientific law which has proved so successful in the natural sciences. But very seldom has an attempt been made to describe how one actually goes about interpreting a case. Here were families in some of which the man had lost status and the student had decided that this loss was due to the fact that the man had become unemployed. What is the meaning of such a statement and how can it be verified?

The problem becomes clearer if comparable examples from daily experience are remembered. The commission which tries to investigate the causes of a railroad accident; the historian who tries to explain a political event—both are confronted by a similar task. They must face the fact that they cannot make a controlled experiment: we cannot take people out of jobs at random in order to see what happens to them, any more than we should care to create a series of different conditions in order to determine when railroad accidents occur and when they do not.

Thus we meet the problem of "the causality of single events" and we have to draw on the fund of our general knowledge to answer the question: "Would this event have happened if a specific factor had not been present?" The section on "discerning" traces carefully all the operations which enter into such a judgment. Wasn't there a trend toward deterioration of family relationships prior to the depression? Were there present factors other than unemployment which could account for the man's loss of status? Can we show the different steps through which unemployment has finally resulted in the loss of authority? By describing in all detail how such questions were answered in sixty cases, material was provided of a kind which in the long

---

* The technique of concrete interviewing has been further applied and developed in a later study by Dr. W. S. Robinson, *Radio Comes to the Farmer* (Princeton University Press, 1940).

run will permit the possibilities and limitations of such analysis to be judged.*

The concrete type of interviewing used and the elaboration of the discerning procedure represent the major methodological efforts of this study. But some further techniques deserve the reader's attention. An interesting check on the reliability of the interviews was furnished by duplicate interviews for six cases. Several months after the first interview a second investigator, who had not read the original interview, reinterviewed the family. The comparison of duplicate interviews is analyzed on pages 153-160.

The use of typological classifications is another point worth noting. While the various classifications were arrived at intuitively, their logic was tested in accordance with procedures described elsewhere.† Thus, for example, three patterns of loss of authority were distinguished in Chapter 2. A scrutiny of these patterns revealed that they constituted certain combinations of two features: the kind of predepression authority, and the kind of change. All possible combinations of these features were enumerated. Then these logical combinations were reduced to a small number of psychologically relevant possibilities, which were compared with the classification intuitively derived.

The field work for this study was finished four years ago, and since that time further research experience permits a more mature appraisal of the procedures used. In two respects the setup of the study could have been improved: one pertaining to the interviewing methods and the other to the selection of cases. It was clear at the outset that information given by one family member would not be reliable enough; therefore at least three members of each family were interviewed, and their reports checked against each other. Another way of increasing reliability would have been to make repeated interviews with the same family member. The first interview, corresponding to the one reported in this study, would have made the respondents aware of the problem. As a result they might have become keener observers of details in the family's daily life;

* This problem, too, has since been explored further. See especially E. Reuben, *A Logical Comparison of a Number of Theories in Explaining the 1929 Depression*, submitted as a master's thesis to the Department of Economics of Columbia University, 1939.

† For a more detailed description of these procedures, which also draws on other studies sponsored by the Institute of Social Research, see Lazarsfeld, Paul F., "Some Remarks on the Typological Procedures in Social Research," *Zeitschrift für Sozialforschung*, VI, No. 1 (1937).

thus a second or perhaps a third interview might have greatly increased the relevance of the observations reported.

In the last few years a number of studies on the effect of the depression have appeared, all of which agree on one point: that the depression has tended to accentuate the psychological framework in which people lived before the depression. Well co-ordinated families tended to draw closer together, whereas families in which difficulties had already appeared were likely to deteriorate still further. It might have been wiser to select cases on the basis of this or a similar hypothesis, according to the principle of deviate cases. If we had taken families who had been well co-ordinated before the depression yet in which the husband had lost status as a result of unemployment; and if we had added families who had had difficulties before the depression but who had improved during the depression, we might have had a setup which, like a microscope, would have magnified the psychological phenomenon which is of main interest here. Case studies are always very expensive and their best use may lie in the analysis of exceptions to general trends, which should first be ascertained by crude statistical procedures.

The two ideas of making repeated interviews and of selecting case studies within a broader statistical framework are two valuable research devices which have developed as a result of the intensive concern with the present study. Thus, in addition to having clarified certain operations which had heretofore been used much more loosely, this study also proved fruitful in giving direction to subsequent efforts.

PAUL F. LAZARSFELD

1

THE FAMILIES AND

THE INTERVIEWS

INTRODUCTION

THE purpose of this investigation is to study the relation between the man's role as the economic provider of the family
and his authority in the family. What powers does the man
have by virtue of being the provider? What effect does the
economic dependence of the wife and the children have upon
their attitude towards the head of the family? How is the
role of this economic factor modified by other features of family
life?

Within its limited sphere of investigation the study thus poses
the important problem of the interrelation between economic
factors on the one hand and social institutions and relations
on the other.

Depression and unemployment provided a tragic opportunity
to study these problems. What happens to the authority of the
male head of the family when he fails as a provider? It is
reasonable to expect that unemployment will tend to undermine
the authority of the husband and of the father. Economic competence is one of the chief grounds of prestige in our society.
In so far as the family shares these social valuations, the
economic failure of the man might tend to lower their esteem for
him and hence his authority. Furthermore, with the family no
longer dependent upon him, he cannot exercise economic coercion
by granting or withholding economic benefits.

1

The unemployed husband's status may also suffer for another reason. In the traditional patriarchal view of the family, the husband is expected to support and protect the wife, and she, in turn, to take care of his household, to honor and obey him. A certain subordination to the authority of the husband is part of the woman's share in their reciprocal relations. In so far as the husband's claim to authority is based upon his supporting his wife, unemployment may tend to undermine it.

Should the study reveal that unemployment tends to disrupt the authority of the man, it may be concluded that the role of the provider was an essential basis of his authority. The reverse, however, is not equally conclusive. If the unemployed man maintains his authority even when he no longer furnishes the means of subsistence, the economic origin of his authority is not disproved. It may be that the man's authority originally derived from economic sources will persist long after he loses his job. Years of economic dependence upon the man may have engendered in the family attitudes and habits of deference which continue even when he fails as a provider. His authority may prevail also because of the strength of patriarchal traditions which have had their historical roots in part in the economic structure of society. Therefore, finding no change as a result of unemployment will not be so conclusive for our problem as positive results.

Using unemployment as a laboratory situation for the study of interrelations between the economic factor and the authority of the man requires additional qualifications. Unemployment is a complex of factors, some of which are, and others are not, strictly speaking, economic. It may bring about increased presence of the man at home or cause other modifications in the family's manner of living, and these changes have their own implications for authority. Thus in tracing the effects of unemployment, we, in reality, trace the effects of a number of conditions more or less remotely related to the economic factor as such. These distinctions are dealt with in greater detail in the body of the report.

While the study is focused upon the effect of unemployment upon authority relations, it may be of interest to the student of the family from a number of points of view. It should add to our knowledge of the structure of the contemporary family. What is the extent of the husband's authority with regard to various spheres of life? What means does a father employ to maintain his authority? How do the cultural stereotypes and personal attitudes interact in family relations? What problems arise because of the discrepancy between the traditional concepts of the roles of husband and wife and the realities of contemporary life?

The changes brought about by the increasing economic independence of the wife are frequently discussed in connection with the family. It is needless to say that inferences from this study must be made with great caution. If we should find that unemployment disrupts the husband's authority through making the wife economically independent, we must not assume that her economic independence in a different social situation would present the same picture of husband-wife relations. The whole foundation of marriage would differ. Nevertheless the study has suggestive implications for this aspect of family life.

The results of the study may be considered from a larger point of view, in their relations to the problem of authority in modern life. To quote from M. Horkheimer, *Studien über Autorität und Familie*, page 900:

"Of all the social institutions which make the individual receptive to the influence of authority, the family must be recognized as the most important. In its circle the individual experiences the impact of social forces. Through it he gets his conceptions of their intellectual and moral content. The family largely determines the role those forces play in the formation of his spiritual life. Moreover, the patriarchal structure of the modern family serves by its very nature as an important preparation for the acceptance of authority in society. . . To be sure, it does not represent any final and independent force, but is a part of the evolutionary process. The social relations which the family helps to preserve and strengthen, themselves constantly reproduce it."

At a time when the discussion between democratic and authoritarian systems dominates political life, it is important to get more insight into the psychological conditions of the two systems. Because the family, as Horkheimer has pointed out, is so important an agent of developing and molding authoritarian attitudes, changes in the authoritarian relations in the family may have far-reaching social implications for the coming generation. Even a partial breakdown of parental authority in the family as an effect of the depression might tend to increase the readiness of the coming generation to accept social change. The particular direction of social change will depend upon a multitude of forces. The breakdown of parental authority might, under some conditions, tend to make young people more self-reliant and strengthen the democratic forces. Under other conditions, the weakening of parental authority might cause the adolescents to look for a substitute and be more susceptible to authoritarian ideas. The section on the effect of unemployment upon parental relations will bear upon these problems, although it is not within the scope of the investigation to pursue the possible social implications of observed changes.

In addition to the theoretical, the study may have some more practical implications. The changes in personalities, social life, and political attitudes of the unemployed, the reaction of the children to the relief status, their outlook on life, all these are matters of concern to many social agencies concerned with the problems of family life in times of depression. Public and private relief agencies, for example, may find in the study some clues as to the effect of certain policies upon family life.

The interest that this investigation may have for the student of methods of research was discussed in the Introduction by Dr. Lazarsfeld.

THE APPROACH TO THE FAMILIES

The families which furnished the data for the study were all residents of a large industrial city just outside New York City. They were interviewed during the winter of 1935-36. Their names and addresses were secured from the offices of the Emergency Relief Administration. In order to secure a homogeneous group the investigators were supposed to give addresses of families with the following characteristics:

1. Parents native-born.
2. Protestants.
3. Head of the family a skilled laborer or a "white-collar" man.
4. Complete families—that is, families consisting of father, mother, and children living together.
5. Families with at least one child over 10 years of age.
6. Families in which father was the sole provider of the family prior to unemployment.
7. The head of the family unemployed for at least one year.

The investigators of the E.R.A. went through their files, copying names and addresses of each successive case meeting the above qualifications. The attempt to keep the group homogeneous was not altogether successful, although most of the families did fulfill the stated requirements.[1]

The families were not informed in advance of the visit of the interviewer. The interviewer rang the door bell and introduced the study personally. Its purpose was explained as an attempt to get the point of view of parents upon the school problems of children, and the general problems of bringing up children during the depression.

In the course of the interview, the interviewer, if asked, enlarged the scope of the study to cover general changes that the depression had produced in family life.

The interviewer, of course, assured the family that no names or addresses would appear on any records. The final report was to publish general conclusions without revealing the identity of the individual contributor.

No immediate practical benefits were promised to the families. It was made clear to them that such good as might come of the study would be in revealing the truth about the experiences of families who have lived through the hard times and know what unemployment means to parents and children.

The families were paid for the interview, $1.00 to each parent and 50 cents to each child. The question of pay was usually introduced in the course of the interview. It was very seldom used as an inducement in case the individual appeared suspicious of the project. The matter of payment was taken up with a statement along the following lines: "We feel that our survey is a worth-while project which people are usually glad to further. But as it takes some time to talk the matter over, the sponsors of the project feel that persons are entitled to some remuneration for the time they give. We have, unfortunately, only a small fund available for this—$1.00 an interview."

The interviews were conducted privately. Three interviews were usually taken in one family—one each with the husband, the wife, and one child, usually the oldest. In some cases it was possible to make it clear at the outset that the interviews were to be private, and to make corresponding arrangements with the members of the family. In other cases the interviewer had to exercise much ingenuity in securing private interviews.

[1] See pp. 134-135 for the composition of the sample.

Interviews with children often took place in a drug store over an ice-cream soda. The men interviewers frequently talked to the men over a glass of beer in a nearby restaurant.

The interview with each parent lasted from two to four hours. The average duration of the child's interview was about one hour. No notes were taken during the interview. They were dictated after the completion of the interview.

The length of a case record for the family varied from 25 to 70 typewritten pages. The average is about 35 typewritten pages.

Of the 89 families approached in the study, 30 refused to be interviewed, and in three cases the interview was given by one spouse while the other refused. In a few cases, the reason for the refusal was serious sickness of a member of the family or some other temporary disturbance. Some persons did not accept the explanation of the interviewer and were suspicious of the real purpose of the survey. Whether the families that were suspicious of the interview had things to conceal is hard to say. It may be supposed that if there were those who had misrepresented their economic assets to the relief authorities, they would be among those suspicious of the investigation. Other persons were disinterested and, in spite of the financial inducement, did not care to take the trouble to be interviewed. The refusal was sharp and angry in a few cases. Others allowed the interviewer to discuss the matter with them and then refused to take part in the survey.

The reaction to the study on the part of the 59 families that consented to be interviewed varied. A few of the men appeared interested in the purpose of the study and apparently proud to have been called upon to cooperate. "People talk a lot about things," they said: "without knowing what they are talking about. It's a mighty good thing that somebody has decided to find out the truth as to how people on relief feel and what problems they have to face."

Others were suspicious and reserved at the outset of the interview, and granted the interview only after repeated explanations and assurances of the interviewer.

The majority of the families, however, seemed drawn into the interview after the preliminary introduction, and only after one or two hours of talking returned to the original question, "But what is it all for?" Some were under the impression that a large section of the interview was just a friendly chat irrelevant to the main purpose of the study.

To summarize, it may be said that the families, while somewhat mystified by the project, felt that it was harmless. It has
been said that human beings in our urban communities are
suspicious and lonely. The reaction of the families to the
interviews perhaps confirmed this impression. When the initial
suspicion was broken down, one found them ready and eager
to talk about their lives. Many times the man or the woman
exclaimed at the end of the interview: "Why I haven't done so
much talking in all my life! I think it has done me a lot of
good."

THE JOHNSONS—ONE INTERVIEWED FAMILY

The interviewer found the Johnson home in one of the run-
down residential districts of the city. It was in a block of
dilapidated frame houses needing paint and new leaders. The
front door bell did not ring, so he went to the back where one
of a group of children playing in the yard told him on which
floor the Johnsons lived. At the top of three flights of stairs he
found the Johnson flat opening into a dark hallway. Mrs.
Johnson opened the door and eyed him with suspicion. The
interviewer hastened to explain that he was working on a survey
of school children. Its purpose was to find out what parents
thought about the school problems of children and the general
problems of bringing up children during the depression. "Are
you selling books?" Mrs. Johnson was skeptical. "Well, if
you're not selling anything, what good is this going to do you?"
Mrs. Johnson was unconvinced, and again the explanation was
given. Finally the interviewer was invited into the flat.
    There were four rooms for Mr. and Mrs. Johnson and their
three children—John 18, Helen 15, and Peter 11. The interviewer was ushered into the parlor, a chilly, unused room, where
he sat down upon a leatherette sofa with cracks in the back. Its
companion piece, an overstuffed chair, stood over by the piano,
and an oak table stood in the center of the room. On the table
stood a vase of artificial flowers, a portrait of Mrs. Johnson's
brother, Joe, in a sailor's uniform, and a green glass ashtray.
Under the table was a well-worn rug. The room was clean, but
cold—so cold that Mrs. Johnson soon asked the interviewer
down the hall to the kitchen. He passed by the bedrooms, filled
with a double bed, a bureau, and a chair. The kitchen was by
far the cheeriest room in the flat, and the only one heated. It
was warmed by an oil stove in the center of the room, and was

filled with chairs, a table, icebox, sewing-machine, radio, canary. Mr. Johnson was shaving over the kitchen sink.

Mr. Johnson guardedly eyed the interviewer. He looked careworn and weary, and older than his 40 years. When the interview had been explained to him, he started to talk about the good old days. He was a carpenter and a good one, even if he did say so himself. He had always felt that he was as good a man as the next, and a good deal better than foreigners and Negroes. One thing he had always prided himself on was paying his bills and taxes on time. And he had always had a good enough job so that his wife didn't have to work. It was terrible the way some men let their wives work, but not he. It wasn't much that he asked for—just a moderately decent living, maybe a home of his own, a chance for his children to get a proper education.

He himself had only gone through the eighth grade, had stopped to go to work, and had married young, but he hoped to be able to do better than that by the three children. He had wanted Helen to finish high school and then go to business college, and the boys to take up a skilled trade after they finished high school. After all, one of the important things in life is to see your children do better than you were able to do. They had been good children, too. It wasn't often that his wife had had to turn to him for help in disciplining them, only when they were really bad. Of course, taking care of the children was really the wife's job, but she had had to turn to him once in a long while, and he didn't believe in "letting her down" when once she had told the children something was to be done.

They were home-loving people. He had never been much of a church man, but Mrs. Johnson had always enjoyed the sewing circle at the First Methodist Church. He had belonged to the Moose Lodge, and of course friends used to drop in for a game of cards and a cup of coffee. Saturday nights they used to go to a movie and have ice cream afterwards.

When the depression came, the building trades "went on the rocks" and there was no work to be had anywhere. He said he would be glad to talk to the interviewer and tell him anything he wanted to know. There was nothing much to say. All the family needed was for him to find work. Everything would be well again if he could find something to do.

Mr. Johnson made arrangements with the interviewer for another meeting, put on his lumber jacket over his frayed overalls, and went out to see if he could pick up some odd jobs—maybe washing windows for the minister's wife.

During this talk Mrs. Johnson had sighed and nodded her head in agreement. She remarked that it wasn't so easy these days to find work when you are past forty the way they were. She had always said that what a woman wanted in a husband was a good steady worker who would support the family and wouldn't drink or go out with other women. Mr. Johnson had always turned the money over to her. In the old days she had been able to pay the grocer, give the children their allowances, and even save a little money from the pay check. It was so much nicer to take care of the house when they had money to heat it and keep the furniture in repair. They used to have such a nice apartment with six rooms, but they had moved three times since then.

Most of the interviewed families were like the Johnsons. They were families of skilled, white, Protestant workers. The parents were between forty and forty-five years of age, with two or three children. The husband, who had been the sole support of the family, had been on relief for three or four years. The income derived from other sources was negligible. The head of the family might earn a few dollars now and then for odd jobs. The 15-year-old son or daughter might make a little money working in a grocery store or running errands for neighbors. The families had moved several times and had lived in their present flat for a year or so.

Before presenting our results we must consider four questions which the reader has no doubt asked himself already:

What is meant by the term "authority" or "status"?

What kind of changes are defined as deterioration of authority?

How to ascertain with any degree of reliability whether these changes have taken place?

How to be sure that the observed changes in the status of the man are due to unemployment?

DEFINITION OF THE TERM "AUTHORITY" OR "STATUS"

The term "authority" is used in this study to mean relative power exercised by one individual over another. The authority of the man within the family refers thus to the relative control which he holds over members of the family.

This definition departs from the accepted usage of the term "authority" in two respects. Authority is usually identified with dominance. Thus, the husband in a matriarchal family is said to have no authority whereas, in our terminology, the husband in a matriarchal family has little authority—little chance of subjecting the family to his will. Furthermore, the term "authority" usually connotes control based upon respect, love, reverence, or at any rate some degree of emotional acceptance of the bearer's claim to power. From this point of view it is contrasted with physical coercion. In this study it was found more expedient to identify authority with control irrespective of its sanctions and grounds. The nature of this control is designated by qualifying terms.[2]

According to this definition, to view a relation between two individuals from the point of view of authority is to consider the relative chance that each has of asserting his will over the will of the other. It can be readily seen that any authoritarian relation involves several elements. It may extend to different spheres of life. The power of one to superimpose his will over the other may be more or less great. Finally, the grounds on which one accepts the control of the other may differ.

CRITERIA OF DETERIORATION OF AUTHORITY

The deterioration of the man's authority was defined as decline in the willingness of the family to accept his control whether or not he succeeded in maintaining it through added coercion. The decline in the willingness to accept the man's authority need not always bring about loss of external control. Whether or not this takes place depends upon the added coercive pressure which the man brings to bear to command the usual obedience. But even if the man succeeds in maintaining control over his family, the relation would be more coercive, more dependent upon external sanctions, and would constitute deterioration of authority.

In the light of this definition, the criteria of deterioration of authority are twofold: (1) loss of man's control over one or

---

[2] Consistency with the above definition of authority often demands that the term be used with qualifying adjectives as "little," "much," "superior." The bearer of authority should be described as the bearer of superior authority. While this usage was generally adhered to, the qualifying terms were omitted in some instances for the sake of simplicity.

In the course of the study the term "status" was used synonymously with authority. For the "ground of the husband's authority" we have sometimes substituted "wife's attitude towards the husband."

more spheres of family relations, (2) changes in grounds of acceptance. In some cases, the decline in status was inferred from some defeat of the man, in others from changes in attitudes of members of the family and still other cases contained evidence of both.

Control must be viewed in its psychological context rather than in the merely formal aspect.[3] The wife may take over the supervision of the children's schoolwork. From their point of view, she may have authority in this sphere, but she may be forced to do so merely because her husband does not care to be bothered and therefore shifts the responsibility to her, perhaps against her wish. In such a situation, what may seem to be the wife's control of the activity, reflects, in reality, the husband's authority.

Since we are concerned with the *loss* of control, it is clear that every defeat in activities of daily life, intimate relations, or the realm of opinion and outlook, must be viewed in relation to the predepression situation. The defeat may be complete or partial. It may manifest itself in some previously existing sphere of relation or in a newly arisen situation. For example, a child who has formerly been willing to submit to the curfew regulation may now fight against it. A wife who has always accepted her husband's control of the financial affairs of the family, now wants to have a greater part in it. This illustrates a conflict in a sphere where, prior to unemployment, there was complete obedience to the man. But the change may be from conflict to complete defeat. Hitherto existing arguments concerning late hours have ceased because of the complete defeat of the father. Now the child comes in whenever he wants to. A Catholic wife and a Protestant husband fought over the religious education of the children. Since unemployment, the wife achieved a complete victory, and the children were transferred to a Catholic school.

Loss of control may also manifest itself in conflict in some newly arisen situation, provided there was submission to the man previously. Now that the father is at home, some conflict may arise over help with housework. The father may insist that the child help with the housework. The child, hitherto obedient to the father, rebels at this new regulation. There is conflict which sometimes results in favor of the child and at other times in favor of the father. The change may be regarded as a

[3] See criteria of dominance, pp. 150-153.

loss in the father's authority due to the more severe tests to which it is put by the new regulations. To take another illustration: the husband-dominated husband-wife relation. Since unemployment, the problem of who should go to the relief office causes conflict. For the first time the wife opposes her husband's will.

In the above-cited examples, the man suffered only a partial loss of authority, as manifested by conflict. However, he may experience complete defeat. The child may refuse completely to help with the housework; the wife may force him to go to the relief office.

It may be argued that defeat of the man in a new situation does not constitute loss of authority. Rather, it shows that the man's authority was not equal to the new demands put upon it. If it were tested by the hitherto existing tests, he would still be able to maintain it. But it is very doubtful, indeed, whether it is true that he would still be able to assert influence over the old spheres. It is much more probable that the challenge to the man's authority and the conflict in the new situation has generally modified the psychological relation.

The last two situations considered conflict or defeat in some newly arisen sphere against a background of complete authority of the man. It is more difficult to classify situations in which new conflicts occur against a background of partial authority. A self-willed child has always fought with his father concerning late hours, associates, and so on. The father has never had much authority. Unemployment caused a new conflict over the child's allowance. The father decided to cut it down and the child rebelled against it. Whether such situations were considered as deterioration of authority depended upon the degree of change. The decision was made on the basis of total evidence presented by the case: indications of changes in attitudes towards the father, his own testimony, remarks of other members of the family, and so on.

So far no distinction was made as to the mode of the man's defeat. If the defeat came after conflict and was the result of the helplessness of the father, it should obviously be classed as loss of authority. But mere withdrawal from exercise of authority was also considered a loss of authority. The whole analysis of criteria of loss was based upon the assumption that the man does want to exercise it. The analysis of the cases justifies this assumption. In general, the desire of an individual for self-assertion and status is greater than what he actually is able to get, and therefore the main problem is always how many of his claims are accepted by his environment and on what ground they are accepted. Therefore, if there is a relinquishment of claims, it is probably a result of pressure and not of a voluntary choice. If a father withdraws from control of the children's lives without conflict, he probably does so because of a feeling of inferiority and anticipation of defeat. However, it is possible, theoretically, that under the plight of unemployment a man changes his outlook upon life. Matters of prestige and status mean less to him, and he withdraws voluntarily from exercise of authority. Such conversions do not, strictly speaking, represent loss of authority, and would require for their analysis a different conceptual framework. No such situations were found among the cases. All cases of withdrawal were apparently forced withdrawals and therefore were put into the loss category.

One interesting kind of withdrawal from exercise of authority requires special mention. There are cases in which the husband and the father chose, apparently, to relinquish some parts of his claim to authority for the sake of safeguarding his authority from complete collapse. The men in such cases gave up their claims to personal service on the part of the family and became more helpful with housework, more attentive in general, more self-controlled. Thus one girl says, "Father used to have a little temper, but now it is impossible to start an argument with him. If you try, he just waits until you are through and pretends he didn't hear anything."

In some cases this relinquishment of claims is consciously motivated by the desire to keep the love of the family. In other cases the dominant sentiment of the man appears to be sympathy for the family and desire to make life easier for them. We have considered such partial relinquishment of claims a loss of authority if there were indications of subtle changes in attitudes. The attitude toward the person whom one serves is not the same as toward one who shares the burdens of the household. When there are even slight indications of changes in the direction of more democratic and equalitarian relations, the case was considered a loss case. Not all cases in which the husband improved in his behavior towards the family were classed as loss cases, although the motivation in his improvement might have been the same. In some cases the wife gives evidences of deep appreciation of the husband's consideration; there is no hint of any deterioration of her attitude.

There are very few cases of voluntary relinquishment of

claims. The interviewing technique may not have been subtle
enough to detect such behavior. On the other hand, it may be
that such behavior is rare. It is well known that the greater
the power and the security of the individuals, the more mag-
nanimous they can afford to be in details. The men in the study
were all in a situation of long-lasting and profound defeat.
It may well be that in such a mood no one is able to renounce
any claims; that, indeed, even the minor situations become
symbols of status. It may be that the unemployed man cannot
avail himself of the psychological advantages which magna-
nimity in details offers to the man who is sure of his status.

So much for loss of control as evidence of deterioration of
authority. Changes in attitudes toward the man were reflected in
statements such as the following:

"When you are not working, you do not get so much attention";
"She gets mad at me when I tell her that I want more love";
"When money goes, love flies out of the window"; "How can
you love a husband who causes you so much suffering? Certainly I lost my love for him"; "I think the children have lost
respect for their father"; "I am afraid the children don't think
as much of me now that I am unemployed"; "The children act
cold toward me. They used to come and hug me, but now I
seldom hear a pleasant word from them"; "If I only had money,
I could make the girl do things for me. Now that I cannot
offer her a nickel for helping her mother with the dishes, there
is no way of getting her to do it."

The changes in attitudes may become apparent from descrip-
tions of specific situations. The wife is highly dissatisfied with
the husband for his unemployment, accuses him of not looking
for work, blames him for hardships that have befallen the
family; the child is increasingly sulky and saucy. In every
case, of course, the testimony of one member of the family is
checked against the testimony of the others.

When blame for unemployment appears against the background of fairly happy family life, it undoubtedly constitutes
a real change in relations. Blame for unemployment means
constant nagging about job-hunting, bitter criticism for family
hardships, bitterness toward the man which will manifest itself
in withdrawing from him the habitual services, spiting him, and
so on.

But a problem arises when blame for unemployment is just
an additional ground in the history of continuous quarreling
between husband and wife or unsatisfactory paternal relations.

Blame of the man was considered proof of loss of status when blame represented a new element in the attitude of the wife or the child, while the predepression relations had been satisfactory, or at least the dissatisfaction on the part of the family had been concealed.

Blame of man was not considered to be proof of change when unemployment was just a new ground for dissatisfaction which had been previously expressed with the same frankness for other reasons.

There is a final question as to how severe a change must be in order to be considered a loss of authority. Certain changes appear too mild to be considered a loss of authority. If a woman says, "Yes, I am more irritable, but it's just from worrying so much. If I say something harsh, I always regret it afterwards. I don't really mean it," and if the husband confirms such a statement, and there is no other indication of change in relations, this growth of irritability in itself on the part of the wife would not be considered as proving loss of authority.

Such are the changes in family relations which were considered as evidence of deterioration of authority. The problem of ascertaining whether or not such changes have taken place and what the role of unemployment was in producing them, is discussed in the following pages.

How to Ascertain Changes in Authority Relations

The evidence of changes came entirely from the testimony of the members of the family. We had no predepression records of the families. A more reliable procedure was followed by Dr. Ruth Shonle Cavan who obtained preunemployment records of the families and followed up the cases during the depression.[4] This procedure has a drawback. The families for which predepression records are available are selected in one way or other and constitute exceptional families. Since we had to depend completely upon the testimony of the family, the formulation of the questionnaire and of the instructions to the interviewers was focused upon the problem of devising indices for ascertaining changes in authority relations.

The success of the whole study depends upon the possibility of solving this problem. Both the questionnaire and the instructions to interviewers were therefore elaborated with great

[4] *Family and the Depression* (Chicago: University of Chicago Press, 1938).

care and may have an intrinsic methodological interest and application for other studies.

The reader who has no special interest in methods may turn directly to page 23.

Authority relations were ascertained not through direct questions regarding who had the upper hand in family relations, but indirectly through an elaborately devised series of *concrete test situations* covering various spheres of husband-wife and parental relations. The interview treats systematically one sphere of life after another: discipline of children, money, sex relations, religious activities, leisure-time interests, relations with in-laws, etc. If conflicts existed in particular spheres, how were these conflicts resolved? If there existed differences in interests or attitudes, whose will dominated the life of the couple?

The advantage of using the indirect approach to authority relations is twofold: First of all, there is less chance of defense and rationalization on the part of the informant; secondly, such systematic inventory of life situations reveals mutual attitudes and behavior with richness of detail and furnishes a basis for interpretation which the informant himself, even if willing, would be unable to give.

It is clear that the selection of the concrete situations must depend upon knowledge of the mode of life of the group studied, its life values, leisure-time pattern, typical conflicts and problems. A study of each particular social and cultural group would require different tests. Take, for instance, a question concerning the attitude of the wife to her husband's smoking. This proved revealing of marital relations in a number of cases. The expenditure for smoking is practically the only personal expenditure of the unemployed man, and it is often symbolic of marital conflicts. In happy families the typical attitude of the wife is, "That is the only pleasure left for him. Why should I nag him about it?" In families with conflict, the wife says, "Smoking is not a necessity. There are things that the children and I need more." The actual practice connected with it, that is, how the money for smoking is allotted, what restrictive effect the wife's attitude has, may reveal the relative status of the husband.

This little test, while occasionally of value in the particular group studied, would be meaningless on a higher income level.

To take another illustration, the radio often provided a concrete test of authority. If members of the family want to listen to different programs, how is the conflict resolved? Does the father's choice take precedence over that of the children's? Does the father complain that he cannot listen to his favorite programs because they conflict with the favorite choices of the wife or the children? Once again it is obvious that using the radio as a test involves the possession of one by the family, and must again, therefore, depend upon the group investigated.

Ascertaining what changes have taken place was, of course, the most difficult and critical problem of the study. How much can the individual remember of the past? How likely is he to distort the past by viewing it through the prism of his present experiences and attitudes? Is there a tendency to idealize the past or, on the other hand, to read into the past such mutual irritations and disappointments as unemployment may have brought about? May there be a tendency to attribute to unemployment conditions which in reality do not represent any changes—that is, conditions that have existed prior to unemployment?

If the study were based upon objective records of the pre-depression situation or if some other form of observation of the family were possible, the study of changes would be less difficult. But our study depended upon the statements of the informants concerning their own experiences. In view of that, the major problem of the interview in ascertaining changes was directed to two goals: how to help the informant reconstruct the past and interpret his experiences as they bear upon our problem, and how to break through deliberate lies or rationalizations.

The following are the techniques which the interviewers used to (a) help the informant tell the truth, and (b) help him to reconstruct the past.

Changes Were Ascertained through an Inventory of Concrete Situations. Changes were ascertained through systematic inventories of spheres of life. The informant was asked to describe concrete situations, and questions as to changes were asked with reference to each.

The order in which changes were ascertained was as follows:

1. What is the situation in specific spheres of life?
2. What changes have occurred since the depression in this particular sphere?
3. Which of these changes are due to the depression?
4. How does the informant know they are due to the depression?

This step-by-step approach assists the informant in recalling the pertinent experiences. It was found particularly useful with children. If the children are asked whether father is stricter than he used to be, or whether they have more or less conflict with parents, they have to review in their minds the present situation and reconstruct the past. If, on the other hand, the child is asked, "Who helps you with homework? How was it when father used to work? Who scolds you when you bring a bad report card home?" and so on through every possible situation, great assistance is given to the child, and the answers can be given in greater detail.

The Direct Questions Concerning Changes in Authority Attitudes Come after the Inventory of Changes in Spheres of Life. We first asked the informant to describe concrete situations in various spheres of life, inferring authority attitudes through them. Only after this were the direct questions asked.

The direct questions in the father's questionnaire (Do children blame father for unemployment? Can an unemployed father command any respect from his children? etc.) come only after an elaborate discussion of parent-child relations in specific situations.

The attitudes of the wife were ascertained in the same fashion. The direct question (Does the wife make it harder for the husband to bear the depression? Does an unemployed husband lose the respect of his wife?) come after the sections in which the husband is asked to describe concrete situations of their daily life.

This order is important for several reasons. The informant may not be aware of authority relations and the indirect questions serve to reveal the unverbalized aspects of the relations. Furthermore, the informant may at the outset of the interview resent the direct questions about intimate and often painful matters. He may be put on the defensive and misrepresent the situation so as to protect his own pride or the good name of the family. Thus, some wives when asked directly "Has your husband really tried hard to find work?" answered affirmatively. Yet these very women, when asked in another connection whether in their opinion they personally might have found work, answered in a few cases: "I think I could find a job. I think anyone who has push and tries hard can find something to do, even in these times."

Some other techniques for ascertaining changes will be quoted from the directions to the interviewers.

1. *If you encounter attitudes, conflicts, relations which by their very character must be affected by the depression, do not fail to trace change.*

ILLUSTRATIONS:

a. Wife has always had to account to husband for every penny spent and was irked by it. With the loss of the husband's earning power a new situation is created: The relief money is not earned by the husband. Has wife taken advantage of this as an excuse to throw off the irksome control of the husband? Does the wife feel that she is entitled to more control over the expenditure of the relief money? Has she finally become more independent of her husband in spending money?

b. Father never permitted children to accept gifts from relatives or friends because he felt gifts spoiled children. Children obeyed him. Does the unemployed father feel that he has no right now to enforce his prohibition of gifts? Do they actually receive gifts even though his own attitude hasn't changed?

2. *Be alert to new situations.*

The changes in authority relations *are more apparent in new situations.* Sheer inertia sometimes maintains the external structure of authority relations in the old and familiar situations. A new situation allows a fresh reconsideration of the authority structure.

ILLUSTRATIONS:

a. The relief situation may furnish an illustration in certain cases. If the husband was the dominant person in the marriage, the authority structure of their daily relations may to some extent be sustained through sheer habit. A new situation is created by the necessity of shopping with relief slips. The husband is humiliated by relief and would prefer the wife to take over this duty. What is her attitude? Does she feel that the least an unemployed husband could do is to spare a wife this humiliation and attend to this himself? How is it resolved? Is he the one to undertake it in spite of his reluctance?

b. Another illustration may be provided by the family's moving into a new apartment. In the old apartment the husband may have had his armchair near the radio, or the best light, or he may have had his desk near the window. Such preferential arrangement may have continued through habit even after his status has declined. A new situation in the new apartment cleans the slate, as it were, and permits the new authority relations to show themselves. This may be discovered by asking the husband whether he is as comfortable in the new apartment as he was in the old one.

3. *Be alert to uncover conflicts.*

    Conflicts, or the way conflicts resolved, offer a good clue to the authority relations.

    Some suggestions for discerning conflicts:

    a. If either husband or wife expresses a preference or an attitude with a great deal of emotion, ask whether the other agrees with him, or her, on this question.

    b. Follow each indication of differences in outlook or personality between husband and wife with a question as to possible conflicts.

    c. Follow up description of some special hobbies or habits, "A cigar is one thing I haven't been able to give up," with question as to the husband's, or wife's, attitude towards it.

4. *Follow up each indication of conflict with a question as to change.*

    Conflicts are likely to represent the most unstable areas of relations and the most susceptible to change. If the revealed conflict refers to the preunemployment era, ask about the effect of the depression upon it. If it is a current conflict, find out whether it existed prior to the depression.

    For example, a woman testified to conflicts with her husband over her expenditures on clothes. He never let her have enough money for clothes. Ask, do they conflict less or more since going on relief? Does she feel freer of his dominance now that the money is not his?

5. *Follow up each statement of change with the possible implications for authority.*

    Thus, for example, the informant testified, "Husband has been taking children to and from school since he is unemployed." This statement in itself is incomplete because this change may have various effects upon the authority relation. Further questions must be asked to ascertain the consequences of this change for authority. Have father and children become closer as a result of this change? Do children talk to father more freely about school affairs? or, Is father irritated by this new task? Do they often have arguments or conflicts on the way? etc.

    In the foregoing paragraphs we described techniques for discerning changes through questions as to change. In some cases these questions refer to specific spheres, in other cases they refer to general attitudes. In addition to this means of discovering change, the questionnaire contained sections pertaining specifically to the circumstances of marriage and the first stages of married life. Age at time of marriage, duration of courtship, attitude of in-laws towards the spouses, expectations at time of marriage were discussed in order to ascertain mutual attitudes and expectations prior to unemployment.

In addition to the instructions described above, the interviewers were trained to require specific answers. One form of specifying questions is the "leading question." Here again we. shall quote from "Instructions to the Interviewer." While it is generally considered that leading questions tend to distort the evidence, there are certain rules which will minimize the danger and make leading questions useful.

1. *Follow up general questions with specific leading questions.* Whenever the informant answers, "I don't know," "I can't think of anything" don't give up too quickly. Suppose the informant, when asked "What aspects of the depression have hit your children hardest?" answers: "I don't know." It is legitimate to suggest possible effects of the depression and to test the informant's reaction to them: Is it lack of money for movies or sweets? Inadequate food? Sympathy for the worries of the parents?

2. *The leading questions should be asked only after the general ones.* It is significant which answers the informant emphasizes of his own volition.

3. *The interviewers should always record which answers came as a response to a leading question.* This may be done by using such short cuts as "No, the children do not mind moving to a new house."

4. *Always insist on illustrations to affirmative answers.* To answer affirmatively is often the line of the least resistance. "Are your children ashamed of being on relief?" It is easy to say "Yes." "What makes you think so?" "They wouldn't go to the grocery with a relief check," or "They asked me not to tell their friends that we are on relief." It is only such illustrations that give validity to affirmative answers.

In order to test the reliability of the questionnaire an experiment was conducted in the course of the study. Families originally studied by one member of the staff were reinterviewed four months later by another. The second interviewer had not read the original interview. The comparison of the five sets of original and duplicate interviews is presented on pp. 153-160. The results of the experiment were encouraging with regard to the reliability of the questionnaire. The two sets of interviews yielded identical conclusions on the central problems: The kind of predepression family relations, and the presence or absence of deterioration in the man's status.

ARE THE OBSERVED CHANGES DUE TO UNEMPLOYMENT?

The preceding pages dealt with the problem of ascertaining whether or not changes in authority relations have taken place.

We now face the second problem. Are these changes due to unemployment? Family relations do not stand still. Changes in authority may have taken place for numerous reasons that have nothing to do with unemployment. This is particularly true of parental authority relations. Unemployment lasted in some cases three or four years. During this period the children have become older, and growth is ordinarily associated with some decline in the father's authority. We cannot assume, therefore, that loss of the man's authority which has occurred in an unemployed family is necessarily due to unemployment.

Discerning whether or not unemployment was the cause of changes was based upon a thorough analysis of each unemployed family. For the sake of convenience, the procedure of determining the casual relation between two variables within a particular case may be termed the *procedure of discerning*. The procedure of discerning is described on pp. 135-145. We have made an attempt to set forth in great detail the mental operations involved in deciding in any given case whether or not loss of authority was due to unemployment. The conclusiveness of discerning for the problem at hand is discussed on pp. 145-146. In a general way it may be stated that the authors attributed loss of authority to unemployment only in cases in which the evidence for the causal relation was fairly complete in terms of principles of discerning.

2

THE BREAKDOWN OF

THE HUSBAND'S STATUS

The Frequency of Breakdown

UNEMPLOYMENT does tend to lower the status of the husband. It has had this effect in 13 out of 58 families included in the study.

TABLE 1

The Extent of Breakdown of the Husband's Authority

	No. of Cases
Loss due to unemployment	13
Loss due to other factors	1*
No change	44
Incomplete	1
Total	59

* In the following tables this case is included with the "no change" cases, since unemployment has not produced any changes in this family.

In some families the hitherto concealed contempt for the husband came into the open; in others unemployment has reversed the husband-wife relation—dominance of the husband having been changed to his complete subordination; in still others the husband suffered a loss of respect, a change which is best described in the words of the wife: "I still love him, but he doesn't seem as 'big' a man."

23

That only 13 families were thus affected may appear to indicate that being the provider plays some, but after all only a small, part in determining the prestige and powers of a husband. It might be pointed out, however, that relief does not completely free the wife of economic dependence upon the husband. The relief allowance is so meager that the husband continues to be at least a potential provider. By taking families on relief we have excluded those now supported by a wage-earning wife. The importance of the economic factor for the husband's status would probably be fully revealed only by such a complete reversal of economic roles. Families in which the deterioration of the husband's status has led to the separation of the couple were also excluded from our study, since we have taken only complete families.

It must be remembered, furthermore, that most of our couples are middle-aged people married for 15 to 20 years. Attitudes become crystallized in marriages of such duration. Even had the prestige of the husband derived in part from his function as a provider, sheer force of habit may protect it for some time against the impact of unemployment.

Finally, it is possible that changes in some of the families have eluded the interviewer. There are undoubtedly such cases. Just how wide the error may be the reader should judge for himself after having scrutinized our methods. The check afforded by three independent interviews and the reliance upon indirect indices of changes make it probable that only the subtle changes or those repressed by both wife and husband have eluded the interviewer.

It will be shown in the discussion of parental relations that the unemployed man's status proved to be more precarious with his wife than with the younger children. Furthermore, it is his authority over the adolescent children which proved most vulnerable to unemployment.

THREE PATTERNS OF BREAKDOWN

To give a general picture of the changes wrought by unemployment in husband-wife relations, we shall present three cases, each illustrating a particular pattern of change. In the first pattern, that of *crystallization of an inferior status*, unemployment has merely made more explicit a previously existing inferior status of a despised husband. Another pattern may be best described as the *breakdown of a more or less coercive con-*

trol. In this pattern unemployment has undermined the authority of a more or less dominant husband over a subordinate and resentful wife. Finally, in other cases unemployment has *weakened the authority of a husband over a loving wife.*

Unemployment crystallized the inferior status of the husband. In families illustrating this pattern the woman dominated the family prior to the depression. Furthermore, she neither loved nor respected her husband.[5]

The depth of her contempt or antagonism for her husband differed from case to case. Thus, Mr. Dorrance was thoroughly despised by his wife for being a shiftless drunkard. Bitter fights characterized most of their married life. Mrs. Baldwin, on the other hand, concealed her contempt for her husband and preserved some decorum in daily relations with him.

The families within this group also varied in the degree of dominance of the wife. In one family the husband was completely beaten. He seldom tried to assert his power. The wife had won all their battles. Her only concession was to keep him in the house. Another wife was frustrated in her attempt to improve her husband's attitude toward the children and to correct some of his other faults. Nevertheless, she had her way in most of the spheres of family life.

Unemployment, in so far as it affected such families, has caused the concealed lack of respect for the husband to come into the open or, if the antagonistic sentiments were openly expressed prior to the depression, to increase the aggression toward the husband. The manifestations of the above changes were in increased conflicts, blaming the husband for unemployment, constant nagging, withdrawal of customary services, sharp criticism in front of the children, irritability at hitherto tolerated behavior, indifference to his wishes, and so on. The story of the Patterson family will illustrate the decline in the husband's status in families in which his position was low even prior to unemployment.

The Patterson Family

	Age
Mr. Patterson	47
Mrs. Patterson	43
Girl	18

Family on relief for a year and one half.

[5] For the criteria in terms of which the various kinds of husband-wife relations were distinguished see pp. 146-153.

Husband-Wife Relations Prior to Unemployment. **Mrs. Pat-**
terson is small, well-built, and still very attractive. She looks
younger than her age. Mr. Patterson is a slight man who talks
quietly and somewhat timidly.

Mrs. Patterson believes she was greatly in love at the time
of marriage, but she said, "You know how those things are—they
never last." She wasn't satisfied with her husband's economic
success prior to unemployment, but neither was she dissatisfied.
While he was a steady worker, they never had enough money to
get ahead on or to have their home exactly the way she wanted
it. She had a couple of girl friends whom she had known for
years, and they had much nicer homes.

Mrs. Patterson gave the interviewer to understand that her
own family was of a higher economic status. Her father gave
her a piano, for example, which she still has, while her husband
could never do that much for *his* girl.

It is clear that Mrs. Patterson dominated marital relations
prior to unemployment. As far as the bringing up of the girl was
concerned, whatever the wife wanted went. She was much
stricter than Mr. Patterson. He was too chicken-hearted; and
if it were up to him, he would never punish the girl. The wife
said, "If you went by his advice, you would be wrong most of
the time." "I could never bring myself to spank the girl," said
Mr. Patterson. "She seldom needed it. She has always been a
very sweet child and still is. But I just left everything to my
wife, because, after all, she had to take care of the girl most
of the time." If the girl asks him for anything he usually
answers, "whatever your mother says goes."

He always turned over his pay envelope to his wife, leaving a
little change in his pocket. Mrs. Patterson worked before the
depression, now and then, to earn money for little luxuries for
herself and her daughter. She helped friends in a store. The
couple used to go out quite often. She usually decided where
they were to go and made dates for both of them. Once a week
he would attend his lodge meeting.

Mrs. Patterson mentioned that she had never been able to stay
at "outs" with her daughter even when the girl was small. She
used to be able to "take anything from her husband," but was
"chicken-hearted" about the girl.

Reaction to Unemployment and Relief. **Prior to the depres-**
sion Mr. Patterson was an inventory clerk earning from $35 to
$40 a week. He lost his job in 1931. At the present time he
does not earn anything, while his 18-year-old girl gets $12.50 a

week working in Woolworth's, and his wife has part-time work cleaning a doctor's office. Unemployment and depression have hit Mr. Patterson much more than the rest of the family.

The hardest thing about unemployment, Mr. Patterson says, is the humiliation within the family. It makes him feel very useless to have his wife and daughter bring in money to the family while he does not contribute a nickel. It is awful to him, because now "the tables are turned," that is, he has to ask his daughter for a little money for tobacco, etc. He would rather walk miles than ask for carfare money. His daughter would want him to have it, but he cannot bring himself to ask for it. He had often thought that it would make it easier if he could have 25 cents a week that he could depend upon. He feels more irritable and morose than he ever did in his life. He doesn't enjoy eating. He hasn't slept well in months. He lies awake and tosses and tosses, wondering what he will do and what will happen to them if he doesn't ever get work any more. He feels that there is nothing to wake up for in the morning and nothing to live for. He often wonders what would happen if he put himself out of the picture, or just got out of the way of his wife. Perhaps she and the girl would get along better without him. He blames himself for being unemployed. While he tries all day long to find work and would take anything, he feels that he would be successful if he had taken advantage of his opportunities in youth and had secured an education.

Mr. Patterson believes that his wife and daughter have adjusted themselves to the depression better than he has. In fact, sometimes they seem so cheerful in the evening that he cannot stand it any more. He grabs his hat and says he is going out for a while, and walks hard for an hour before he comes home again. That is one thing he never did before unemployment, but he is so nervous and jumpy now he has to do something like that to prevent himself from exploding.

Mrs. Patterson says that they have not felt the depression so terribly themselves, or changed their way of living so very much.

Changes in Husband-Wife Relations Since Loss of Employment. The wife thinks it is her husband's fault that he is unemployed. Not that he doesn't run around and try his very best to get a job, but he neglected his opportunities when he was young. If he had had a proper education and had a better personality, he would not be in his present state. Besides, he has changed for the worse. He has become irritable and very hard to get along with. He talks of nothing else, and isn't interested in anything else but his troubles. She and her daughter try to forget troubles and have a good time once in a while, but he just sits and broods. Of course that makes her impatient with him. She cannot sit at home and keep him company, so that during the past couple of years she and her daughter just go out together without him. It isn't that they leave him out—he just isn't interested and stays at home.

Mr. Patterson insists that his child is as sweet as ever and always tries to cheer him up, but the tenor of his conversation about his wife is different. She does go out more with the daughter, leaving him alone. He cannot stand it, worrying so and having them so lighthearted. "When you are not bringing in any money, you don't get as much attention. She doesn't nag all the time, the way some women do," but he knows she blames him for being unemployed. He intimates that they have fewer sex relations—"It's nothing that I do or don't do—no change in me—but when I tell her that I want more love, she just gets mad." It came about gradually, he said. He cannot point definitely to any time when he noticed the difference in her. But he knows that his advances are rebuffed now when they would not have been before the hard times.

The wife gives the impression that there might have been some decrease in sex relations, but declines to discuss them. She tells the following episode:

The day before the interview she was kissing and hugging the daughter. "I like to keep the girl sweet and young, and in the habit of kissing her mother good-night." The father walked in and said, "Don't you get enough of that?" Mrs. Patterson went on at great length as to how terribly that statement hurt her.

The interviewer also witnessed another episode. Towards the end of the interview with the wife, the husband walked into the living room and asked his wife if she thought the interviewer would be interested in talking to their neighbors. The woman said, "Don't bother us, we are talking about something else just now." He got up quietly and went into the kitchen. In a moment she called after him, "Oh, you can sit in here if you *want* to." Nevertheless, he stayed in the kitchen.

Summary. The evidence on the basis of which change was said to have taken place is as follows:

Husband's, wife's, and daughter's statements that wife goes out without the husband more frequently than before, despite his protests.

Wife's statement that she blames husband for unemployment and her dissatisfaction with the changes in husband.

Husband's statement that there has been a decline in sex relations on the initiative of his wife, indirectly supported by wife's testimony.

Husband's sense of deep humiliation at being supported by his wife and daughter.

Unemployment undermined a more or less coercive control exercised by the husband over the wife. This group of wives was also characterized by absence of love or respect for the husband. But these husbands were stronger than their wives. His dominance was accepted with resentment varying from deep hatred to milder antagonism. A few cases were included in which there was continuous conflict between husband and wife with no clear-cut dominance of either. These conflicts meant that the wife could not get a permanent and secure victory and, therefore, resented her husband for frustrations in the regions of conflicting interests.

In so far as unemployment affected these families, it resulted in partial or complete emancipation of the wife from the husband's coercive authority. In some cases the relations were completely reversed; the dominance of the husband was changed to his complete subordination. In other cases the husband suffered defeat in particular spheres. Thus a Protestant man married to a Catholic refused, in spite of his wife's persistent efforts, to send the children to a Catholic school. After two years of unemployment the children were transferred to a parochial school. "After two years of unemployment I just could not fight her any longer," said the husband.

The pattern of breakdown of coercive control will be illustrated by the Adams family.

The Adams Family

Mr. Adams	60	Girl	19
Mrs. Adams	49	Boy	17

Family on relief for two years.

Husband-Wife Relations Prior to Unemployment. Mrs. Adams was a hard-working factory girl 29 years old when she met Mr. Adams. He was 40 years old, separated from his wife and three children. They were married after an acquaintanceship of four months.

"Four months," suggested the interviewer, "is not a very long time to find out about a person."

"You said it," answered Mrs. Adams. "I would never have married him had I known what was to come. His mother used to tell me, 'You knew what you were getting,' and I said, 'How was I to know? I saw him take a glass of whiskey now and then, and that was all.' "

The first period of married life was very difficult. There were two main problems: Mr. Adams' heavy drinking and his mother. Mr. Adams spent a good share of his weekly wages in the saloon. He was dominated by his mother, who took a great dislike to Mrs. Adams. Mrs. Adams said in the interview that his mother opposed marriage for economic reasons. He was bringing in money, and his mother liked money a lot. She did not want to see any of it go out to another woman. Besides, Mr. Adams' children by his first marriage lived with his mother. His mother was afraid that Mrs. Adams would want them, and that she would thus lose the weekly income which she received for the support of the children.

Whatever may have been the causes, Mrs. Adams' mother-in-law said to Mr. Adams soon after marriage, "You're a fool to have gotten married. You could have had all the booze and all the women you wanted."

Mrs. Adams suffered from economic hardships and from the ill treatment by his relatives. She was quite helpless against her husband. He would take his mother's word against hers any time. She would just cry, but couldn't fight him. She remembers how she used to pay the fare for the taxi that brought him home drunk. If this happened now, she would never pay a cent. The only reason she did not leave him was that she was quite alone in this country, and had no one to turn to. She was born in England, and all her relatives were there.

Mr. Adams' story as to the past relations confirmed the account given by his wife.

Reaction to Unemployment and Relief. The family suffered many ups and downs in its economic life, even before the final unemployment. In 1926, Mr. Adams lost his job because of drink. Since then he has gone into several more or less unsuccessful ventures. From 1930 on Mrs. Adams contributed to the family income as a superintendent in an apartment house, taking in boarders, selling doughnuts and vegetables. Since 1933 the family has been on relief. The family's income is at present secured partly from boarders, partly from the small earnings of the two children. (It is doubtful that the family is entitled to relief.)

Mrs. Adams doesn't know what to say about the effect of the depression because in the last five years she has been more secure than in any other period of her life. When the family applied for relief she insisted on getting the relief check herself. She also controlled the money that was coming in from the boarders and from the children. Thus, for the first time in her life she knew exactly how much she had instead of just getting what was left after Mr. Adams' saloon bill was paid. She doesn't feel the humiliation of being on relief and is quite well satisfied with the present status.

Mr. Adams confirms Mrs. Adams' story of his work history. He feels that he could certainly get a job if he were not so old and sick. He attributes his broken health to heavy drinking. About relief and unemployment he says this: "I want you to put it down in black and white the depression in my case is due to drink."

Changes in Husband-Wife Relations. Mr. Adams said, "There certainly was a change in our family, and I can define it in just one word—I relinquished power in the family. I think the man should be boss in the family. I have old-fashioned ideas on the subject. I tried to be boss in the beginning, but you can't be boss with an English wife. But now I don't even try to be boss. She controls all the money, and I never have a penny in my pocket but that I have to ask her for it. The boarders pay her, the children turn in their money to her, and the relief check is cashed by her or by the boy. I toned down a good deal as a result of it. How did it all come about? Very simple. I stopped earning money, and most of the money that was coming in was coming in through her. Well, I'll be frank with you. Maybe if I had listened to her a long time ago we would have been better off now. But it certainly is hard—the hardest thing in the world is never to have an extra cent."

According to Mrs. Adams, the most important change in the family since unemployment is that she controls the money, and that Mr. Adams doesn't have any to get drunk on. The interviewer witnessed the following episode:

At the conclusion of the interview with Mr. Adams the interviewer put his dollar on the table in the presence of Mrs. Adams. She picked it up and said, "This dollar is mine, just as I told you." Mr. Adams did not argue about it, but as he was on the point of leaving he said to Mrs. Adams, "I have to make a telephone call to So-and-so." She gave him a nickel. "I need some cigarettes." She gave him fourteen cents. "Well, tomorrow I have got to get up early and finish repainting the kitchen." Mrs. Adams said, "No you won't; there are other things to do."

Control over money is not the only change in the family. The sweetest victory for Mrs. Adams is her revenge over her mother-in-law. Her mother-in-law has no home now, and lives first with one and then another of her children. When her turn came, Mrs. Adams refused to take the mother-in-law in.

The interviewer heard the following exchange of words between the two:

Mrs. Adams said to Mr. Adams: "You always go to your mother in preference to me."

He answered, "Do I now take mother's advice in preference to yours?"

"Well," she said, "not now, but you used to, and you would have been better off if you had stopped long ago."

There are other ways in which Mrs. Adams has the better of her husband. They have some differences of opinion about the son's working, but the boy does what Mrs. Adams wants him to do. If she wants to buy some furniture, she just goes ahead and buys it. If he says anything, she tells him it is her money, not his.

Mrs. Adams is sorry she got wise so late in her life. "If I had only not been so soft in the beginning. If I had only set my will against his. But there was no use trying before." If she had insisted on taking his wages away from him when he was earning, she is sure he would just have deserted the family and she would have been left with the two children.

"How does Mr. Adams take all this?" asked the interviewer. Mrs. Adams answered, "He still wants to be boss. That is his nature, even though he knows it wouldn't be for the best. He says he is treated like a dog in the house, but that's not true. He is good for a time, but once in a while the old trouble returns. Last week he came home drunk. She didn't know where he got the money. He didn't have much. He can't stand much now —it makes him sick. She thinks he got drunk last Saturday as revenge, because she said she wouldn't have his mother in the house. He is a very revengeful man. He came in and she didn't talk to him. That doesn't work with Mr. Adams. He goes right out of the house and gets drunk. So he started out of the house and she met him at the saloon door. She got hold of him and started talking to him, and just took him away by the hand.

He cursed and pleaded but she brought him home just the same. It was the first time she got him out of the saloon. Why hadn't she done this before? He would not have stood for it before; he just wouldn't have paid any attention to her.

Summary. The evidence for changes in husband-wife relations is as follows:

Mr. and Mrs. Adam's statements as to Mr. Adam's complete relinquishment of control over money since the family went on relief and Mrs. Adams started to contribute to the support of the family.

Mr. and Mrs. Adams' testimony as to the change in Mrs. Adams' relations with her mother-in-law.

Mr. Adams' statement that he relinquished control in the family.

Mrs. Adams' statement, with various illustrations, that she was too soft before, but has asserted her will in recent years.

Unemployment lowered the status of a loved and respected husband. The first two cases described the effect of unemployment upon what might be generally described as unsatisfactory marriages. The third pattern refers to marriages which were characterized by some love and admiration for the husband or, at the very least, by the absence of any very serious dissatisfaction on the part of the wife. A few marriages in this group were indeed far from harmonious. Thus, for example, one husband was irresponsible, unfaithful to his wife, and an indifferent father. The couple quarreled frequently, the wife complaining of his negligence and cruelty to her. But she continued to be deeply in love with him and was ready to forgive him at the slightest sign of improvement.

As to the relative status of the husband, this group of families consisted of all kinds; in some the husband was the true head of the family, others were dominated by the wife. But, while the woman was the matriarch, the husband accepted her leadership without apparent humiliation or hostility. He was a satisfied husband and thought his wife had good sense and was a good wife.

The decline in the husband's status took the form of the husband's defeat in certain spheres of the marriage relation. In another family subtle changes in the attitudes of the wife resulted in more equalitarian relations in a family hitherto led by the husband. The story of the Holman family will illustrate this pattern.

The Holman Family

Mr. Holman	37	Girl	18	Boy	10
Mrs. Holman	40	Girl	14	Boy	2

Family on relief for two years.

Husband-Wife Relations Prior to Unemployment. Mr. Holman is a young-looking and active man. He is not very intelligent, but he is good-natured and sociable, the kind who must have been the life of the party in "the good old days." He is, on the whole, a good family man. He must have been well adjusted to his job as traveling salesman of hardware articles. This job, while not putting too much demand upon his intellect, provided an outlet for his social interests. Mrs. Holman looks older than her husband. She is a thin and a fretful little woman, but a tireless housekeeper and a devoted mother. She is somewhat more "genteel" than her husband. Mr. Holman tells the following story of their courtship, which, in a way, gives a clue to their predepression relations:

"I was the one for having a little fun. Even when I courted her she would always want to stay at home or go to some quiet, dark spot where there wouldn't be any people. I think she was self-conscious as to how thin she was. Once I went out with another girl—a pretty one—and she asked me, referring to Mrs. Holman, where did I get such a skeleton. That was the end of that girl, because I really loved Mrs. Holman. She was good to me—really like a mother. And she still is."

Their married life was very satisfactory prior to unemployment. It is true that Mrs. Holman was more economical and less sociable. They did not have conflicts over it, because Mr. Holman earned good money, and besides, his work took him away from home for several days of the week.

Mrs. Holman was deeply in love with her husband. She apparently admired him, too. "He is certainly quick with his head. He knows the hardware business. Sometimes I would take the hardware manual and just call out any page and he would tell me exactly what was on that page."

No conflicts existed in this family. Mrs. Holman's attitude was maternal, while her husband's sentiments were those of gratefulness for her devotion. Both were devoted to each other and to the children. She admired him enough to consult with him about various decisions. With regard to money, or children, or church going, there seems to have been a good deal of consultation and joint decisions.

Reaction to Unemployment and Relief. Both Mr. and Mrs. Holman are mystified about the unemployment situation. Their economic philosophy does not offer them an adequate explanation in terms of external factors. Neither do they blame Mr. Holman. At first, Mr. Holman thought of it just as a stretch of bad luck that might turn any day. It was a reassurance to know that this bad luck was of a general character. Mr. Holman said to Mrs. Holman now and then, "I found out today that the So-and-sos are on relief. Well, I guess we're not the only ones. If such people as they are on relief, perhaps we shouldn't talk."

Mr. Holman reacted to unemployment with tireless search for work. He was active all day looking for odd jobs, washing windows for neighbors, and what not, or helping Mrs. Holman when he had nothing else to do. He is a man who likes to brag a bit and does not admit defeat so easily. But with continued unemployment he had periods of discouragement. "He doesn't say anything," says his wife, "but I know he gets so discouraged at times he begins to worry whether he will ever get a job again, we have been on relief so long."

Mrs. Holman does not blame her husband in the slightest for his unemployment. She does not understand why such an energetic and bright man cannot find a job. Depression has been hard on the family because they have been forced to move into a two-room, backyard apartment and deny their children many necessities. Especially is it hard for their eldest daughter, an undernourished, nervous, genteel little girl, who is a senior in high school and deeply humiliated by the plight of the family.

Changes in Husband-Wife Relations. The major conflict since unemployment is over social life and is described by Mr. Holman as follows: Mrs. Holman is of a much quieter disposition and does not like amusements at all. When she spends 15 cents on a movie, she is so worried that she does not get any fun out of the movie. They decided to celebrate New Year's Eve. They got some one to stay with the children and went to a movie and had coffee and sugar buns afterwards. When they got back she said, "Now that it's done, I wonder if we wouldn't be better off to have used the money for some of the things we need." But he is different. He likes good times. But they have conflict even when the amusement does not cost any money, because Mrs. Holman is jealous. For example,

they broke up with their best friends because she was jealous
of the woman for no good reason at all. The Holmans used to
meet with the other couple, and the woman would just "kid" and
dance and make merry, and Mrs. Holman would sit and sulk in
a corner. Sometime ago, Mr. Holman joined a WPA club.
He thought he could get a job through them. Well, they drank
a bit. Once he came home late and she was furious. Mrs.
Holman confirms this story. She says that they are of different
temperaments. She likes to stay at home and he likes a good
time. She confirmed her irritation with regard to the club. "It
isn't right for a married man to stay out so late, is it? Besides
why should he have a good time and spend money when I am
going crazy trying to make ends meet on a relief allowance?"

All of these conflicts were resolved in Mrs. Holman's favor;
Mr. Holman no longer attends the club and they stopped seeing
their friends. The conflicts have arisen as the result of unemployment because, as Mr. Holman explains it, in the past he
had had his share of good times on the road away from the family. Furthermore, Mrs. Holman could not use their poverty
as an excuse to restrain his social life. At the present time,
whenever he suggests some recreation that might cost a few
pennies, she invariably reminds him of the manifold needs of
the family, and this is the only time she speaks of his unemployment with a hint of reproach.

The evidence for changes in the husband's status is as follows: Unemployment has given rise to new conflicts between
husband and wife. Some potential disagreements came into the
open, and the strength of the husband's authority was put to a
new test. The wife emerged as a victor out of this "tug-of-war."

This general description of the breakdown of the husband's
status will be followed now by the discussion of the process of
change as it bears upon two questions: which aspects of unemployment proved decisive in the deterioration of the husband's
status, and what was his own reaction to the change.

The Various Ways in Which Unemployment Led to the Loss of the Husband's Status

Unemployment is a complex of conditions, and it affected the
status of the husband in a variety of ways. This was clearly
revealed in the attempt to discern the relation between unemployment and the changes in the attitudes of the wife. Not all

aspects of unemployment were equally disruptive of the husband's status.[6]

In some cases unemployment affected the husband's status because of the loss of earning power. The husband could no longer control the wife as heretofore by granting or withholding economic benefits.

The *weakening of economic coercion* occurred in cases in which the wife did not love her husband and tolerated him as a price for advantages of marriage. We do not assume, of course, that every time the wife deferred to her husband's wishes she was consciously aware of the possibility of his withdrawing support. It is only with the children that it is as simple as that. The father says, "I'll give you a nickel if you will go to the store for me," or, "If you don't behave, you will not go to the movie." With the wife, economic coercion exists as a general background of adjustment in marriage.

Loss of earnings and failure to provide for the family affected marital relations in still another way: they *lowered the prestige of the man* and lessened the respect that the wife had for him.

Possession of money carried with it power and prestige, but it apparently played still a third role in marriage. For some husbands *money has provided a margin of tolerance,* an area within which his authority was not put to severe tests because conflicting interests could be satisfied. Loss of money has narrowed this area, and for the first time necessitated choices and hence created new tests of the husband's authority.

[6] The aspects of unemployment which, through discerning, were linked directly to the change in the wife's attitude were called the decisive features. If the analysis shows that the wife felt free to give vent to her contempt for her husband because she was no longer afraid to lose his support, the decisive features may be described as "loss of money as a means of control." In another case, the change in the wife's attitude may be traced to changes in the husband's behavior. As a result of loss of a job the husband became irritable and his behavior antagonized his wife. When the change in the attitude of the wife came at the end of a chain of events, the decisive feature was defined as the one immediately leading to it—in this case, changes in the husband's personality. Economic failure and loss of money may also operate in this case. But they account for the changes in the husband and so belong to a different line of analysis, which will be taken up at another stage of the investigation. In some cases the deterioration in the wife's attitude is a progressive process and can be linked directly to more than one aspect of unemployment. The man's failure as a provider and his growing irritability both are shown to have affected the wife's attitude. In such cases the decisive feature was defined as the *initial* blow to the husband's authority.

It is not always possible to decide which of these three economic aspects of unemployment was the decisive feature in a
given case. It is particularly difficult to decide whether weakening of economic coercion or loss of respect as a result of economic failure of the man was the critical element in the case.
Economic coercion takes subtle forms and is seldom admitted
by the wife. If the husband loses his earning ability and with
it his power, the wife is likely to rationalize the change in terms
of the man's lack of responsibility for the family. Furthermore, change in the behavior of the wife as a result of both
aspects of unemployment may take similar forms. Take for
example the Baldwin and Patterson families. In both of these
cases we find more open contempt for the husband, less consideration for his wishes, quarrels with him over unemployment. Mrs.
Baldwin, prior to unemployment, controlled her irritation with
her husband over his lack of interest in "education." After unemployment she did not hesitate to call her husband a "big
lug," who, because he failed to make something of himself, was
the cause of all their suffering. Mrs. Patterson had always been
disappointed in her husband, but never treated him with as
much contempt as since his loss of employment.

The change might be explained by various processes. Both
Mrs. Baldwin and Mrs. Patterson may have, even in the past,
felt as much resentment and contempt for their husbands as
they do now, but restrained the expression of their sentiments
because they owed their livelihoods to their husbands. Now
they are free to talk. We might say that in such cases the
change was due to the weakening of economic coercion. But
another explanation is possible. A husband who was an insurance salesman with a small income may have been a big disappointment to Mrs. Baldwin, but an unemployed husband can
command still less respect. In most cases, no doubt, both
existed because one was likely to merge into the other. It is
probably true that the very fact of economic power endowed
the husband with some prestige. The wife may have thought,
as did Mrs. Garland, that her husband had no personality,
but after all she recognized the fact that the house, the car, her
clothes, and the summer vacation were derived from him. This
fact in itself must have endowed him with some prestige.

In still another situation, economic failure of the man has
apparently provided the wife with a convenient way of rationalizing her dissatisfactions hitherto concealed. It is less dis-
turbing to Mrs. Baldwin's conscience to blame her husband for

lack of education now that this lack can be held responsible for his failure as a provider. It is easier for the dissatisfied wife to rationalize all kinds of grievances in terms of unemployment. She seizes upon his unemployment as a socially accepted mode of voicing grievances which she had had to conceal prior to unemployment. It is not merely that the wife finds in unemployment an acceptable pretext for voicing her dissatisfactions; she feels freer to voice them now that the man holds no economic whip over her.

Increased presence of the husband at home affected his authority in two ways. In some cases it led to disillusionment in the husband. Apparently, authority depends upon distance and absence in certain kinds of relations. Mr. Fucini says that "when a man is at home all day he cannot possibly command as much respect as when he returns to the family for a few hours of concentrated conversation." The husband feels that he is a "fallen idol" to his family, and attributes it largely to his presence at home. His wife has become more aware of his little weaknesses. As for the children, they used to meet him in the evening with a glad welcome, and now that he is at home all day they don't pay any attention to him. Now when he comes in, they sometimes call out, "Hi, Dad," and again they may not even do that.

Increased presence at home meant also that potential differences and disagreements of husband and wife came into open conflict and, in some cases, resulted in the defeat of the husband.

Most wives testify to the increased irritability and conflicts due to the man's presence at home. These exist even in families which do not show any changes in authority relations. Conflicts that arise through daily contact are of all kinds. One husband does not approve of the wife's housekeeping. She likes to work and rest alternately, while he thinks that she should complete her duties before resting. Another frequent source of conflict is over the children. Now that the husband is at home all the differences in the attitudes of the couple come to the foreground. The disagreements might be over the eating habits of the children; whether or not the daughter should help with the housework; whether the baby should be taken out of the crib when she cries; whether the boy should be locked out of the house when he is naughty; how late the children should be allowed to play out of doors—and so on.

The husband's share of household duties is another source of irritation. Now that he is idle most of the time, how much should he be expected to help his wife? There may be conflicts over the hobbies of the husband, or the radio—the man likes speeches and his wife likes jazz. Another man gets so engrossed in a book that he doesn't pay attention to anybody for hours, which irritates his wife. In another case, the wife never wipes the dishes before putting them away, and that annoys her husband. Underlying it all is the deep anxiety of both husband and wife, which increases their nervousness and irritability.

While increased irritability is observed in most cases, in itself it does not imply a change in the husband's status unless the marriage was without conflict in the past, in which case the mere presence of conflict would testify to a kind of rebellion on the part of the wife. Ordinarily, however, increased conflict means that the man's authority is put to a severer test, and thus provides a fertile soil for disintegration of authority.

The fact that the unemployed man spends so much of the day with his family does not always undermine his authority, but it has other unfavorable effects. Again and again would the complaint be made by both husband and wife that his continuous presence at home puts a great strain upon their relations. Work relief is superior to money relief from this point of view as it is also in many other respects.

Changes in the man as the cause of his downfall were the most difficult feature to discern. The relation between changes in the man and changes in authority relations is a complex one. Changes in the man's personality may affect his relations with the family, and changes in his relations with the family may affect his personality. One man may become panicky as a result of unemployment and lose his sense of security and dignity. This is likely to result in behavior which endangers his status. He may become apathetic or he may become overdominant and difficult to live with. Another man may keep his self-respect and equanimity, thus having a greater chance to preserve his authority. But while the man's behavior affects his family relations, the attitude of the family may in its turn affect his behavior. If a family, after four years of unemployment, would not sit down to the table without the man, no matter how late he might be, as is the case in one family, it goes a long way towards keeping up his morale.

The interviewer enters somewhere in the midst of this process and is confronted with the difficult problem of discovering the decisive feature in this circular causation. In assigning the initial cause to the changes in the man, the testimony of the whole case was taken into consideration. The analysis of the material reveals that in three cases the impetus to loss of authority apparently came from the man himself; that is, from changes in his personality.

One such case is presented by the Scott family. "Before the depression," said Mr. Scott, "I wore the pants in this family, and rightly so. During the depression I lost something. Maybe you call it self-respect, but in losing it I also lost the respect of my children, and I am afraid I am losing my wife." But there is other evidence than his own testimony that the decisive feature in deterioration of his status was his own reaction to unemployment, his broken morale and loss of self-respect. Mr. Scott is a man who feels that when he ceased providing for the family he lost all claims to their consideration. An individual who has this view would relinquish his authority as a result of unemployment before it was put to a test. He became discouraged and apathetic. After the first year of relief he withdrew from contact with the children and let his wife handle the financial and other affairs of the family. In the early days of unemployment the children kept asking him to play with them, but because of his constant refusal and irritability they gave it up. He spends most of the day in the corner candy store and has ceased to look actively for work.

An interesting case is presented by the Wallace family. In this case, as in the preceding one, such loss of status as occurred also came as a result of changes in the husband's personality, but the changes themselves were different. It appears in this case that the husband more or less consciously chose to relinquish some parts of his claims for the sake of keeping the love of his family.

In the Wallace family both the wife and the daughter testify that the man has become more helpful to the family and more self-controlled. The girl said that before the depression if you asked him something, he would say, "It's your problem." Now he tries to help. He used to have a temper, but now you can't start an argument with him. He just waits until you are through and pretends he didn't hear anything. "He has become, somehow, more subdued," his daughter said. In discussing his own reaction to unemployment, Mr. Wallace said that he might have become more irritable, but he tries to control his irritability so that his family will not get disgusted with him.

The present family relations are affectionate and both the wife and the daughter are devoted to the man. The wife does not blame her husband for unemployment, thinks he is a very good husband, and would certainly have married him even if she had been able to foresee unemployment. The daughter says that if she could be in love with a man as her mother is with her father she would marry him even if he were on relief. If the husband's authority has declined in the family, the change has certainly not been radical. Nevertheless, subtle changes in the wife's attitude have probably occurred. The concessions that he has made—the control of his temper, the unwillingness to enter into an argument, greater helpfulness—are accepted by the wife without any special sense of gratitude. Furthermore, she talks a good deal about encouraging and consoling him, while in the past his attitude was more self-confident and self-assertive. In the absence of any proof to the contrary, it appears that the observed changes resulted from limitations that he put on his claims.

In summary, it must be stated that the downfall of the husband was due most frequently to the loss of his earning power. In three cases out of the thirteen, the change, it is true, came as a result of the deterioration in the husband's personality and his continuous presence at home. Had he been able to preserve his own morale, had he found some occupation that would keep him away from the family for part of the day, the attitude of his wife might not have changed. But in most of the cases the unemployed man was doomed by the very fact of unemployment. It was not his own reaction to his plight, neither his increased contact with the wife, but his failure as a provider and loss of money which undermined his status. Loss of earning ability has lowered the prestige of the man in the eyes of his wife. He could no longer hold the economic whip over her, and finally loss of money necessitated new choices and created new tests of the husband's authority.

As will be pointed out in the discussion of parental relations, the unemployed father has more control over the fate of his status than the unemployed husband. This is especially true with the younger children. A father who has kept his self-respect has a good chance of keeping the respect of his children in spite of his failure.

It is not to be supposed that the economic factor plays no role in cases in which the breakdown came as a result of changes in the husband's personality. If we were to investigate the manner in which these changes came about, we would certainly find that they were the result of the man's own reaction to his failure as a provider. Thus, whether directly or through giving rise to certain conditions, the economic factors played the major roles in every case of loss of status.

The unemployed husband who has suffered a loss of status with his wife is a tragic figure. Defeated in the outside world, he feels the ground slipping from under his feet within the home as well. What does he do, faced with a crumbling world? Does he struggle to maintain his authority, or does he relinquish all claims to it? With what means does he attempt to arrest the disaster? What escapes and compensations does he seek?

THE HUSBAND'S REACTION TO HIS LOSS OF STATUS

The men did not relinquish easily their claims to authority. They fought bitterly to maintain them in the face of the growing contempt and rebellion of the family. Most men reacted to the loss of status in husband-wife relations as they did in the case of parental relations, by *demanding* that their wives continue to respect them. There was less physical violence and aggression towards the wife than towards the child, because physical force presupposes some power which the man is more likely to have over the child than over the wife. Such pressure as the husband exerted was psychological rather than physical.[7]

The struggle for status took various forms. It manifested itself in part in the increased "touchiness" and in overemphasis of his authority. The husband frequently becomes sensitive to the slightest threats to his status. Incidents which would have passed unnoticed now arouse his anger. Again and again the wife testifies that the husband became "bossy," that he "flies off the handle" at the slightest remark, however harmless. Apparently his sense of insecurity is so profound and ever-present that he views the most trivial incidents of daily life in relation to his status, and these incidents become to him symbolic of his status. The commonplace and familiar activities take the form of contests for status. The wife asks the husband to go and fetch the coal; she complains about the long waiting at the relief office; she tells of a relative who secured a good job; she asks her husband to call for the child at school; the dinner is not ready at the usual time; she is late from a visit with her relatives; she remarks about the torn curtains. His anxiety

---

[7] It is not to be supposed, of course, that all of the behavior of the men is consciously designed to uphold authority. It was in part a spontaneous manifestation of humiliation and anxiety and only in part deliberately calculated to protect his status.

and insecurity make every incident a reminder of his defeat and a hidden threat and insult to which he reacts with irritation and bitterness. As one man put it, "My ears have become sharper. I hear too much. I take things to heart which before I wouldn't have even heard."

Increased stubbornness is another frequent kind of reaction. It seems as if the husband picks himself a few strongholds and does not yield power within them even though he may have been defeated in the fundamental areas of life. It appears as if a refusal to concede to the wife's wishes is a source of satisfaction to the man as a remnant of power over her. In part, it may be sheer spite, a way of avenging himself for the indignities showered upon him. Thus, Mr. Fucini admits the loss of his authority. His reaction to his wife's patronizing and domineering attitude is a withdrawal of customary services in the home. He refuses to help the wife with her heavy housework and in spite of his increased leisure is less helpful than he was prior to unemployment. Mrs. Roland once told her husband not to come home without any money. He says that he was lucky and earned some that day. Yet the wife is quite helpless against his stubbornness in one or two of their daily conflicts. He refuses to tend the fire, he refuses to do errands for her. She says that he won't be budged if he says "No."

It is perhaps not without significance that these strongholds frequently concern help with the housework. Housework is so closely identified with the woman's rather than the man's role in the family that performing it is a symbol of degradation.

Needless to say, such means of preserving authority as those described above do not achieve their end. Indeed, they get the couple into a vicious circle of quarrels and mutual irritation. Mrs. Fucini is disgusted with her husband's refusal to help with the housework while he is hanging around the house all day with nothing to do. In her exasperation she strikes at what she intuitively feels is his most vulnerable spot—she blames him for failure to provide for the family. This in turn deepens his bitterness and anxiety and makes him still more antagonistic to her demands.

Even the casual visitor to the home can sense the bitter undercurrent beneath the apparently trivial exchanges of words between the couples.

The wife might apologize to the interviewer for her shabby dress. (To the husband it means, "My husband failed as a provider.")

He remarks, "You might at least wash it and keep yourself looking decent." (To the wife his remark means "You're not a good housewife, and you're careless about your personal appearance. You're not attractive as a woman.")

The wife says, "Who should I keep myself fixed up for?" (Her husband interprets this as, "You're not a man in my eyes, and I don't have to try to please you.")

A very different reaction to loss of marital authority is one in which the husband attempts to placate his wife through increased helpfulness. Mr. Baldwin, while always helpful to his wife, is now completely at her service during the day. He hopes that his helpfulness will earn for him some gratitude from his wife. When his wife accuses him for his failure as a provider, he defends himself by reminding her of his complete devotion and helpfulness in the home. "There is nothing I wouldn't do for you, and you know it."

Mr. Holman also tries to appease his wife by helping her with housework. In a comparable situation Mrs. Baldwin's answer was, "If you were an office man and had a job, you wouldn't have to do it yourself. You could hire help for me."

The husbands described so far had one thing in common. Whether through aggression or increased services, they nevertheless strove to defend their hurt egos. Of 13 husbands, 5 have ceased to struggle. They may have occasional spurts of rebellion, but these spasmodic efforts do not change the general picture of relinquishment of authority.

Mr. Adams says, "There certainly was a change in our family, and I can define it in just one word. I relinquished power in the family. Now I don't even try to be boss. She controls all the money, and I never have a penny in my pocket but that I have to ask her for it."

Undemanding as these men are as a general rule, they do occasionally attempt to assert their power. Thus, Mr. Adams once in a while secures some money from somewhere and gets drunk in the old style. The wife says it happens after quarrels, and he does it as revenge. Now and then he tells her that he is treated worse than a dog in the family, but this does not happen often.

The humiliation within the home drives some men to seek compensation outside it. It might be remembered, incidentally, that sometimes the man finds compensations within the family. There are several cases of loss of authority over the children, but complete preservation of it in husband and wife relations. The reverse is very rare. There are only one or two cases in which the man has lost the respect of his wife while still maintaining authority over the children, though he may, of course, continue to receive certain sympathy from them. Where such situations exist the man finds solace in some members of the family from the antagonism of others.

In contrast to such compensation within the home, in the Dorrance family the man sought solace outside the home.

The marriage of the Dorrances was most unsatisfactory even prior to the husband's unemployment. The husband was apparently a shiftless and lazy man who had never been able to keep a job. The family accepted charity during the various periods of married life even prior to his final layoff. Bad as it was, there were indications that his unemployment made things still worse. Sex relations have been discontinued for the past three years. The husband said that the wife poisoned the children against him and criticized him in front of the children more violently than she ever did before. This was his reaction to it:

"Well, I'll tell you," he said to the interviewer, "after a while you get so you don't care a damn any more, and that's the way I feel. As far as I am concerned the kids can do what they please, and the wife, too, for that matter. It's just like I said, 'Love flies out of the window when money goes.' "

Mrs. Dorrance confirmed the picture of her husband's indifference. Towards the children, however, he is cruel. He flies into a rage at the slightest provocation, beats the children, and throws things at them. One of the children may be talking, and the husband will tell him to shut up, for no reason at all. If the child happens to be in the middle of a sentence, he naturally finishes it, but even this little delay causes her husband to go into a fit of rage, and he will throw something—a plate, for example—at the child. The children have learned to duck very quickly, and so he has never very seriously hurt any of them.

But while Mr. Dorrance is a "home devil," he is a "street angel." According to his wife, he can be very nice to other children. He always drank some, but during the last few years drinks more than ever before. The little money he has, he spends on being "a good fellow" in saloons. He spends more money in the saloons than she does on clothes for herself and the children. She suspects that he is unfaithful to her.

Leadership of a Holy Roller congregation and respect of its members compensates Mr. Brady for the loss of authority with his children. Mrs. Brady was always deeply religious, but was dominated by her more worldly husband. He was quick-tempered and repeatedly unfaithful to her. Since the depression, the marriage relation has not deteriorated, but the man lost all authority over his children. After about a year of unemployment, the husband was "saved" by becoming a Holy Roller. In fact, he became a leader of the church and spent a good deal of his time in church activities. While the man feels that "my word is not law around here any more"—referring to his children—he is respected by the congregation. His wife says that he was saved "because of many years of her prayers." That her prayers were rewarded after the first year of unemployment is no doubt significant. The interviewer remarks that this man appears resigned to his failure with the children, and talks of his church with a sense of importance and pride.

Mr. Tice found an outlet in organizing the unemployed. He stressed the fact that he was the secretary of the club and was responsible for better service to the members of the club on the part of the local relief office. In fact, he can usually get into the relief office without waiting because of his position.

The vicious circle of the conflict in which the couple find themselves is another striking feature of the process of loss. There are numerous illustrations of the circular and cumulative character of conflicts. Unemployment calls forth some action or attitude on the part of the husband. The wife reacts to it in a manner which aggravates the original attitude of the husband. He hits back, and so the two are caught in a mounting wave of bitterness.

As will be pointed out, families in which no change in the marriage relation has taken place do not get involved in this cycle of conflict. There are conflicts, but one or the other of the spouses fails to take up the gauntlet. The reaction is such as not to call forth the hot retaliation of the other. The wife might complain of unemployment, but the husband, instead of avenging himself upon her for this reproach, tries to justify himself or console her for her hardships. The husband may be irritable and unfair to the wife, but she, instead of seizing unemployment as a weapon to hold over him, tries to alleviate his anxiety. Needless to say, such differences in the methods of conflict are in themselves results of personalities and preunemployment relations of the couple.

But the most striking fact, perhaps, concerning the reaction of the husband to loss of authority is that there are no cases in which the husband has completely accommodated himself to the new authoritarian relation. There is no case in which the husband and the wife have adjusted themselves completely to the realignment of power. The decline in the husband's status is satisfactory to none. Even Mr. Adams, who confessed that it would have been better for the family if his wife had had her way prior to his unemployment, is not really adjusted to his new status in the family. The occasional spurts of rebellion testify to this fact. The one exception is presented by the man who partially relinquished his claims to authority. A subtle change in relations has taken place, but to all appearances there is satisfactory accommodation to this change on the part of both the husband and the wife.

3

PREDEPRESSION HUSBAND-WIFE RELATIONS AND THEIR
EFFECT UPON THE STATUS OF THE UNEMPLOYED MAN

THE breakdown of the husband's authority described in the preceding chapters has taken place in only one-fifth of the families. In the majority of the cases, whatever other consequences unemployment of the husband may have had for family life, it has not changed his relative status in husband-wife relations. What determines the fate of the husband's authority during his unemployment?

Why does Mrs. Garland tell her husband not to come home without money, and say, "When a husband cannot provide for the family and makes you worry so, you lose your love for him," while Mrs. Meyer, after four years of unemployment, does not sit down to dinner without her husband, no matter how late he might be? One wife says, "Of course I hate my husband for bringing hardships upon the family." Another wife comments, "I don't know how I would have stood the depression if it had not been for my husband's encouragement." In the Adams family, unemployment reversed the relative position of the spouses and gave Mrs. Adams the upper hand. In the Dorrance family, the husband's control over the wife has not been undermined.

Among the multitude of factors which undoubtedly affect the fate of the husband's authority during unemployment we have selected for discussion only a few. There are undoubtedly equally important factors which we have not considered because the material was not available or because it was not possible to devise satisfactory criteria.

49

The first factor to be considered is the predepression husband-wife relations. For the purposes of this study it was found desirable to classify husband-wife relations as they existed prior to unemployment.

CLASSIFICATION OF PREDEPRESSION HUSBAND-WIFE RELATIONS

Husband-wife relations were classified in terms of two features: the relative authority of each spouse, and the attitude of the wife toward the husband (or the ground upon which the husband's authority was accepted). With respect to the first feature, families were divided into three groups: those dominated by the husband, *patriarchal;* those dominated by the wife, *matriarchal;* and those in which there was no clear-cut dominance of either. The last group was termed *balance of power* families.[8]

As to the grounds upon which the husband's authority was accepted, three kinds were distinguished. *Instrumental* grounds refer to authority accepted for utilitarian considerations, because of fear, or a combination of the two. *Primary* grounds refer to authority derived from love or admiration of the husband, or from traditional acceptance of the husband's authority. Finally, in the case of *mixed* grounds, authority is maintained, as the term itself suggests, upon a combination of instrumental and primary grounds.

In the light of these characteristics, the following types of predepression authority were distinguished among the 59 families included in the study:

Type 1. Primary attitudes, husband dominant
(or balance of power) .... 27 families
" 2. Primary attitudes, wife dominant .. 8 "
" 3. Instrumental attitudes, husband dominant (or balance of power) .... 6 "
" 4. Instrumental attitudes, wife dominant 6 "
" 5. Mixed attitudes, husband dominant
(or balance of power) .... 11 "
" 6. Mixed attitudes, wife dominant .... 0 "
Incomplete .... 1 "
—
59

[8] The concrete criteria in terms of which each case was classified are elaborated on pp. 146-153.

"Husband dominant" and "balance of power" families were grouped together because in all respects significant for our problem these two types were identical. The detailed summary is as follows:

> Marriages dominated by the husband .. 22 cases
> No clear cut dominance of either ...... 23 cases
> Marriages dominated by the wife ...... 14 cases

The concepts of instrumental and primary grounds must be discussed further before the classification can become clear. In *instrumental* authority the bearer of authority acquires or keeps his status by satisfying some interests that are quite independent of the bearer himself. A child might obey his father's command because the latter promised him a toy. The wife might acquiesce to the demands of the husband as a price of economic security. A child will obey his father who stands over him with a whip. While there are significant differences in the above situations, the bearer of authority in no case constitutes the object of the interests served by the authoritarian relations. The interest may be desire for physical comfort, survival, health, or economic security. It happens that conditions are such that these interests can be satisfied only through some submission to the bearer of authority.

The distinctions between utilitarian and fear authority are in their respective sanctions and grounds of acceptance. In utilitarian authority, economic or other utilitarian interests of the object of authority constitute the motives for acceptance. The penalties for insubordination are economic privations or other disadvantages. In fear authority, the object submits because he is afraid of the bearer. The simplest illustration of fear authority is coercion. In such a case threat of bodily harm is the ground of acceptance. Threat of physical violence is not the only stimulus to fear which may become associated with an infinite variety of objects, persons, situations. For our purposes the criterion is a subjective one, that is, the experience of fear on the part of the object of authority. Whenever acceptance of authority is derived from such fear, it will belong to the category of fear authority.

In contrast to the instrumental, *primary* authority stems from love and admiration of the bearer of authority, or from traditional grounds. The authority of the beloved person may be accepted for various reasons: because of confidence in his wisdom and competence; desire for his happiness; desire for praise and love; pleasure in the submission. In hero worship, the element of adulation is strong. On the other hand, a person may love another without feeling that the loved one is wholly wise and good. Love of a person in spite of his deficiencies, indeed sometimes with conviction of his complete worthlessness, is a frequent theme in song and fiction.

It may be argued, perhaps, that even in primary authority the bearer of authority is a means for satisfying the needs for response or for love. Yet in such a case the object of the need involves the personality of the bearer. The distinction between primary and instrumental authority is not the distinction between ends and means. In primary authority, the bearer also satisfies a need. The only authoritarian relation which is an end in itself is one in which submission is a source of pleasure. The point is that in primary authority the bearer of authority is the means of satisfying some end which involves him, his happiness, his response.

Acceptance of authority based on love and admiration is only one kind of primary authority. Another kind is the authority based on traditional grounds. Certainly, authority relations within the family are determined by institutional patterns. In so far as it survives, the patriarchal pattern endows the husband and the father with some authority. A child accepts the authority of the father not merely because the father is physically stronger, a source of economic benefits, wise, or kind, but because he was brought up in a culture which demands obedience to one's father. The acceptance of traditional patterns is a complex psychological phenomenon. It involves several components. In a strongly patriarchal family, the wife and children may accept the authority of the husband, because of unquestioned acceptance of the culture pattern, or for fear of breaking mores sanctioned by their own conscience or public disapproval. But whatever the origin of these patterns or the psychological mechanisms through which they work, in so far as they exist they constitute a kind of primary authority.

It is not claimed that the above classification of grounds has significance for all types of investigations. For the study of political life or development of authoritarian attitudes in the individual, other classifications would, no doubt, be of greater value.

Psychologists and particularly psychoanalysts would undoubtedly consider the classification too crude. They could maintain, for example, that primary authority may cover quite diverse attitudes. Apparent love and respect may be a part of very different psychological constellations. Love derived from dependence or insecurity has a different meaning from love without any loss of self-assertion. Presence or absence of repressed hostility would also distinguish kinds of primary authority.

While it would have been desirable to study further the primary and instrumental authority, different techniques from those we were in a position to employ would be required to reveal such distinctions as the above. A more refined analysis would throw light on the differences *within* each of our types but would not invalidate the conclusions arrived at by the comparison of the types.

In reality no relations are of the pure or "ideal" type. Thus, for example, a purely patriarchal authority relation does not exist. The attitudes and practices prescribed by the patriarchal pattern may have very different emotional meanings in various relations. The acceptance of the patriarchal authority may be associated with hostility or love or both. The exercise of patriarchal authority may be benevolent or sadistic. Similarly, fear may be an element in many emotional attitudes: reverence, hatred, awe. Indeed, a particular family relation has, no doubt, elements of all kinds of authority. Nevertheless, *concrete authority relations may be dominated by one or another ground*. It was possible, therefore, to group families in terms of the *dominant* ground.

The question may be raised as to whether this classification can be made with any degree of objectivity. The reader is asked to examine the criteria in terms of which the families were classified before deciding this question (see pp. 146-153). After the criteria were formulated, two readers who had not read the cases previously judged a number of the cases independently. The results are as follows:

Identical judgments .... 12 cases
Different judgments .... 3 cases

In the three cases the disagreements were in terms of one interval. Three cases judged to be primary by the first reader were called mixed cases by the second reader.

Before showing how the unemployed husband fared in various types of families, we shall consider separately the predepression attitude of the wife in its relation to unemployment.

THE PREDEPRESSION ATTITUDE OF THE WIFE TOWARD THE HUSBAND

Striking differences in vulnerability to unemployment appear among families classified according to the wife's attitude. The role of the husband as provider is a significant buttress of his authority in some, but not in other, kinds of families. When the ground of the husband's authority was primary, the family showed a remarkable stability in the face of unemployment. It appears, thus, that *unemployment does not so much change the sentiments of the wife towards the husband, as it makes explicit the unsatisfactory sentiments that already existed prior to the depression.* Out of 35 cases of primary attitudes only 2 show deterioration of the husband's authority. Out of 12 cases of instrumental attitudes 8 show loss. Mixed attitudes are intermediate between the two extremes; out of 11 cases 3 show loss.

TABLE 2

WIFE'S ATTITUDE AND THE EFFECT OF UNEMPLOYMENT

	Number of Loss Cases	Number of Unchanged Cases	Total Number of Cases
Primary..........	2	33	35
Mixed...........	3	8	11
Instrumental......	8	4	12
Totals........	13	45	58

These results may be questioned on two grounds. It may be maintained that the classification of the predepression attitudes is faulty because the families affected by unemployment may have tended to portray the past in dark colors. The section on the criteria of attitudes (pp. 146-150) describes the ways in which we have attempted to safeguard against the danger of introducing the effect of the depression into the classification of attitudes.

Furthermore, it may be maintained that a wife who had loved her husband would repress changes in her attitude. She would keep up the fiction of "ours is a happy marriage." It is possible that these wives may have concealed their disappointment even from themselves. However precarious such husband-wife relations may be in the long run, the fact remains that at present there is no overt conflict, criticism of the husband, and other manifestations of loss of status. In other words the changes would be subtle, and would not be registered in terms of our criteria of loss of authority which reflect probably only the more pronounced and overt changes.

The stability of primary authority is quite striking. Primary authority was defined as authority based upon love and respect. Neither love nor respect for the man could, of course, show such immediate susceptibility to unemployment as instrumental attitudes. Unemployment does not strike as directly at the root of primary attitudes. Nevertheless, it might have been expected that even primary authority would, under some conditions, be affected by unemployment: economic failure of the man might lower his prestige and hence admiration for him, and perhaps his sexual attractiveness. Changes in his personality might cause tension and irritation with him, and so on. According to the results of the study, however, this is not often the case.

Love and admiration apparently generate safeguards against the deterioration of the husband's status and offset the defeat of the husband implied in unemployment. In a few cases the attitude of the wife was such *that unemployment was not interpreted as a reflection upon him.* The blame was put elsewhere—upon the economic system, luck, or what not. It appeared that the wife has such admiration and love for the husband that she sincerely felt his loss of a job to be no indication of his incompetence but rather a commentary on the injustice of society or fate.

Such complete faith in the husband as to place him above the tests of economic competence is, of course, rare. In a greater number of "primary" families it appeared that there was *such satisfaction with the husband that his defeat in the economic sphere, although admitted, did not make enough difference to change husband-wife relations.* Against the background of the whole relationship—habits of common life, general advantages of marriage, dependence upon the husband's companionship, perhaps even an increased need of it in times of hardships—the fact that the husband could not keep a job was not important enough to disrupt relations.

The wives with primary attitudes express themselves as follows:

"This depression proves to me how courageous and devoted my husband is to the family. He will go without food for the sake of the children. Besides, he is big and handsome and intelligent and has never looked at another woman since we were married. Much as I love my children, I would be more likely to leave them than to leave my husband."

"Why should I blame my husband for unemployment when I know there isn't anything he wouldn't do for the family if he could only find work?"

"My husband looks for work mighty hard. He is never home except when it rains real hard. He never gets discouraged. He handles everything—the relief and the creditors. Believe me, I'm mighty thankful for that. If it hadn't been for him and his calm ways, I don't know what I would have done. It's an awful thing to say, but I've thought many times of taking gas. If my husband hadn't been so wonderful, I think I would have."

"Money isn't everything; when you get a husband who is as good to you as my husband is to me, you can certainly consider yourself lucky."

"My husband is not a millionaire, but he is a good husband and a good father."

There is still another way in which primary authority may deter change. Confidence in the wife's devotion may contribute to the preservation of the husband's morale and thus indirectly of his authority. There are many illustrations of actions of the wife which safeguarded the personality of the husband. Thus, Mr. Olsen says, "My wife is a good psychologist. I noticed that when I get irritable with the children, she always takes them over to a neighbor and gives me a chance to calm down." In another family, the wife, who was employed for a short time, showed great tact in making her husband's dependence on her as painless as possible. She let him pay the rent and generally disburse the money. She introduced him to the people she worked with. The wife of one unemployed truck driver is an excellent housewife and works hard to make the most of the relief allowance. On a cold winter day she refused to let her husband go out and look for work. "He might as well stay at home and keep me company and go out the next day." In the Foster family the wife never asks her husband upon his return whether he has found any work—waiting for him to tell her whether or not he had had any luck.

So much for primary authority. In a case of utilitarian authority, the wife will tolerate the husband because he is the provider, and because of the general social security that marriage gives. She may acquiesce to some demands even of a despised husband, because she realizes subconsciously that rebellion may cost the total security of her married life, disruption of the home, scandal of a separation, ill effect upon the children, solitude, and so on. Of course, not every marital conflict is visualized in terms of these alternatives. In daily life, the woman's subordination to or tolerance of the man takes the form of desire to keep the peace, or simply helplessness against the man's stronger will.

Unemployment, impinging upon a situation of that sort, would naturally tend to undermine the authority of the man. One of the main grounds of instrumental authority is the economic advantage, and it is precisely this that unemployment eliminates. Indeed, one might ask why unemployment does not completely disrupt marriages of this sort. As a matter of fact, we know that it has done so in some cases, although the exact extent of such breakdowns during the depression is difficult to ascertain. But it must be remembered that separation calls for a major decision, and is resorted to only in extreme cases, because the pressure is always on the side of continuing a marriage. In the Dorrance and Jones families, after several years of unemployment, the wife still hopes that the husband will resume work and that she will be better off than if she had to depend upon relief for herself and her children. Furthermore, habit and the social advantages of marriage are also deterrent to change. In addition, there may be religious scruples, or a sense of duty to stick by even an unemployed and incompetent husband.

The cases grouped under instrumental authority included also some cases in which fear of the man was present as an additional element to utilitarian authority.

We have only two cases of fear of the husband. These husbands are violent, forceful husbands, who overpower their wives. Neither of these cases shows change. Perhaps when the wife with instrumental attitudes has no fear of her husband, unemployment affects his status more immediately.

Our study does not permit a comparison between fear and primary authority. It would seem that fear of the man would provide a more unstable situation with the duration of unemployment than primary authority. First of all, fear of the husband presupposes some preservation of his morale. He must assert his will with some violence and assurance. Prolonged unemployment might undermine his strength. Secondly, the wife's realization that he is an economic failure, that he has no claims upon her, that she does not depend upon him economically, may all cause a rebellion at his domination.

In so far as mixed authority involves a combination of primary and instrumental elements, it presents no new theoretical considerations.

We can turn now to the joint consideration of ground and dominance and see what additional light is thrown on preservation and loss of authority by viewing the types of husband-wife relations in their relation to our problem.

TYPES OF HUSBAND-WIFE RELATIONS

The joint consideration of ground and dominance throws additional light only on the instrumental types because the number of cases is small. According to the following table, when the wife's attitude was instrumental, the weak husband suffered loss of status more often than one who was stronger than his wife:

TABLE 3

INSTRUMENTAL ATTITUDES AND THE EFFECT OF UNEMPLOYMENT

	Loss	No Loss	Total
Instrumental, matriarchal..................	5	1	6
Instrumental, patriarchal or balance of power..	3	3	6
Total instrumental..................	8	4	12

When we compare the cases falling into the two types, we find that while in both types the wife had no admiration or love for her husband, in one the husband was the stronger of the two spouses. The greater power that the husband had over the subordinate but resentful wife apparently stood him in good stead when he became unemployed. In the case of the weaker husband, on the other hand, nothing kept the wife from giving vent to her contempt for, and irritation with, her unemployed husband.

Among the primary cases, the relative dominance of the man might well have the opposite effect from that observed in instrumental types. The number of cases is too small to prove it, but the analysis of a few cases suggests that *within primary authority the matriarchal families may show greater stability than those dominated by the man.*

In matriarchal families, the whole marital life was characterized by the husband's dependence upon the wife. Unemployment did not present so great a break in relations. For the wife who had no illusions about her husband, who did not idealize him, but who loved him in a protective and maternal way, the failure of the man to secure a job may not be much of a change. The wife, in a patriarchal family, on the other hand, had looked up to the husband. It may be that the admiration for the husband will survive the shock of unemployment, but the relation is more precarious.

In the preceding sections we have compared the relative stability of the unemployed husband's authority in various types of husband-wife relations. The analysis of the cases suggests additional hypotheses with regard to certain variations in the wife's attitudes. The criteria of these grounds were too difficult to formulate to warrant counting.

ADDITIONAL HYPOTHESES AS TO THE EFFECT OF THE WIFE'S ATTITUDES

The Role of Patriarchal Traditions. Is a family dominated by the patriarchal concept of family life more or less stable in the face of unemployment than the modern individualistic family? Would the husband's authority in an Italian immigrant family, for example, prove more or less resistant to unemployment than his status in an urban individualistic marriage? What is the relative vulnerability of authority attached to the office of the husband as compared with that derived from personal interaction of the married couple and other circumstances of a nonpatriarchal family?

The salient features of the patriarchal pattern include the clear-cut specialization of the roles of husband and wife—husband the provider, wife the homemaker; the subordination of the personality of the wife to that of the husband; the supremacy of the husband's will and interests over those of the wife; the duty of the wife to defer to her husband, and of the husband to provide for his wife and protect her.

In the cultural group in which the patriarchal pattern is not so strong, the office of the husband is not endowed with authority. The wife in such families will not accept the dominance of the husband as his prerogative. The authority relations in such a family will be worked out, as it were, anew, without the traditional predetermination. If the husband is dominant in such a family, it would be by virtue of other factors than institutional prerogatives: wife's economic dependence upon him, love for him, physical coercion, dominance of his personality, and so on.

Let us consider first those aspects of a patriarchal family which may make it more vulnerable to unemployment. The patriarchal pattern views marriage as a reciprocal arrangement in which it is the man's duty to provide and the woman's duty to accept his dominance. Might it not be reasonable to expect that this view would make the husband's status unstable now that the man is no longer a provider? The patriarchal family may be vulnerable in still another way. It may be reasonable to expect that a man brought up within the patriarchal pattern may be less adaptable to changes brought about by unemployment. He would have a greater sense of inferiority as a result of the change in his role as a provider, and he would find it more difficult to modify his role within the family.

On the other hand, there are certain conditions that would tend to make the patriarchal family more stable. If the pattern was deeply rooted in the emotions of the wife, subordination to the husband may continue through habit. Other things being equal, this is just one more force tending to maintain the husband's authority. Furthermore, the woman in a patriarchal family is likely to have less sense of personal independence and a weaker sense of alternatives to marriage. She would not, even in the face of economic failure of her husband, have the feeling that she could get along without him. It may also be that patriarchal families are likely to be the more religious ones, and have the sanction of religion to stick by the husband "for better or for worse." The wife in the patriarchal family may, in general, live by tradition, and have less of a habit of rational calculation of benefits derived from marriage. Thus, even if there is no love for the husband, the wife in a patriarchal family is more likely to accept her fate. She will also be the one whose traditional attitudes would be strongly opposed to divorce.

It may be possible to disentangle these mixed effects of the patriarchal tradition if the wife's attitude towards the husband is taken into consideration. The following generalization may be suggested.

If the man is not loved or respected by the wife, if he has no personal leadership, the presence of a stronger patriarchal pattern may make the family more stable. The weight of tradition will be just one more factor deterring change.

On the other hand, of two families in which the husband is loved and admired by the wife, the nonpatriarchal one may be the more resistant to change. It would seem that the role of the provider would be a more important element for the patriarchal family. Its disruption will disorganize the whole concept of the husband's role and prerogatives. For the wife who admired and loved her husband for personal qualities and was not brought up in strongly patriarchal traditions, his role of provider may be less intimately tied up with the whole complex of her attitudes.

Unfortunately the whole problem must be left in the realm of speculation because of the difficulty of isolating the role of patriarchal traditions. The cultural group to which the families belonged was homogeneous, so that the variations in patriarchal traditions were relatively small. It is true that some women and men talked of their marriage in terms of patriarchal stereotypes, as, "I would not think of asking my husband to do housework," "I would rather starve than let my wife work." In other cases there was no mention of these stereotypes. But it is impossible to know to what an extent these verbal statements reflected a real conditioning to patriarchal patterns or were merely used as convenient rationalizations.

The difficulty of isolating the role of the patriarchal pattern and distinguishing it from personality configurations, will be illustrated by the comparison of the Wilson and the Page families:

The Wilson family illustrates a patriarchal family. The husband is the kind who says, "The woman's place is in the home. I would rather starve than let my wife work." The wife says, "It isn't a man's place to help with the housework."

On the other hand, the Page family seems a perfect example of an equalitarian family. The husband assumed part of the household duties because he loves to cook, enjoys housework, and likes to finish work together with his wife so that they may enjoy their leisure together. He makes fun of the husband whose pride is hurt by housework. His notion is that marriage is a partnership, and whatever needs to be done must be done by both.

Up to the present, no indication of change in either of the families is apparent. There is some reason to suppose that the Wilson family, should unemployment continue, would be the first to be affected, and if that happens, it will be mainly through the change in the man's personality. Mr. Wilson is already much more worried about his status, although there is apparently no objective reason for it. He feels that he is failing in his duty as a man, and can hardly expect the same attitude from the members of the family towards him.

One possible interpretation may lie in the following sequence: Man brought up to a rigid patriarchal conception of man's role—unemployment affects this role—he cannot adapt himself to changes because early conditioning made him identify this role with self-respect—he loses self-respect or compensates in some undesirable fashion—this affects family relations.

The sequence in the Page family was presumably as follows: Man brought up with less stress on the patriarchal role—unemployment changes his status as a provider, but does not strike as deeply at his self-esteem—he adapts himself to the changes, takes up housework, for example, because this is not identified with his self-esteem as a man—his adaptability, in turn, tends to preserve family relations.

However plausible these sequences may be, the truth may lie elsewhere. It may be that the difference between the two husbands lies, not in the strength of early conditioning to patriarchal mores, but in their relative need of them. Suppose both of these husbands were brought up in the same cultural milieu. It would still be possible that one would be adaptable and modify his traditional role without undermining his self-respect, while the other would insist upon it, cling to it, and feel insecure without it. Suppose, for example, that the couple in the Page family is well adjusted sexually. The husband may not have the same psychological need of his institutional role as a provider. He may have the assurance that in spite of his failure as a provider his wife still needs him. Mr. Wilson may lack this assurance. Other factors than sexual adjustment may operate in the same way. Whatever will make a man insecure as to his ability to maintain status within the family, will make him apprehensive of the loss of the institutional prerogatives of a husband. It is thus difficult to ascertain in any given case whether patriarchal mores are the true explanation, or just a way of rationalizing some inferiority feelings.

The Timid and Fearful Wife. Among the marriages in which the wife is dominated by her husband and her attitude is mixed, there are some that present a special interest for our problem. Those are the couples in which the wife is a weak and submissive woman, dominated by the husband and showing some antagonism towards him, or at least confessing major areas of conflict in which she is defeated. In contrast to instrumental cases, these wives do express some respect and love for the husband side by side with hostile sentiments.

Mr. Smith is a stern, stubborn, domineering man who might

bully even a stronger woman, but his wife's submission to him is characteristic of her behavior in other situations. She is a person who, in general, lacks self-confidence and self-assertion. Once she went into a barber shop that advertised an especially cheap haircut. As she sat down, she discovered that the advertisement was misleading and misrepresented the price. Although she could hardly afford the price asked, she had no courage to contest or even to question it.

Her husband, Mr. Smith, is a stubborn, revengeful, narrow-minded man, who imposes upon the family a number of oppressive policies. Mrs. Smith, who suffers under these policies, does not, however, put up a fight against them. Being a timid person she has no confidence in her opinions and decisions. When Mr. Smith expresses forcefully some decision, she, even though it may be for the moment only, begins to doubt her own objections and is overwhelmed by the force of his self-assurance. But even if she is sure that her own stand on some of the children's requests is the correct one, she has no courage of her convictions, no courage to witness her husband's dissatisfaction. She accepts his decisions because it is easier for her to do things she personally disapproves of than to face his anger. That is true even in trivial daily affairs. Mr. Smith usually decided upon the menu for the family dinners. Mrs. Smith would like to suggest a meal sometimes, but she seldom does it because she has no courage to face her husband's possible dissatisfaction. It is easier for her to eat a meal she doesn't like than to have to defend her choice against his displeasure.

In rare quarrels between the spouses, Mrs. Smith defends herself with tears rather than with indignation. Her lack of confidence in her own opinions, in her ability to handle situations, undermines the indignation that she might feel at certain of her husband's acts.

Because of the deep-rooted fear and timidity that characterize Mrs. Smith's personality, her husband does not need ultimate sanctions to impose his will. He does not need to show anger. Even the slightest sign of displeasure suffices. She is very sensitive to his moods. She is always afraid of hurting his feelings, partly, no doubt, because she projects her own sensitivity, knowing how easily she gets hurt, but also because she fears his displeasure—to hurt him is dangerous. To have him displeased is a threat to her and not merely because of his attitude towards her. She has learned, to depend upon him, and when he is sulky or unhappy her security is threatened.

Mrs. Smith expresses admiration for her husband in spite of her disapproval of some of his actions. She thinks him a very handsome and attractive man, intelligent and capable. Whether her insistence on his good qualities is motivated by the need to idealize the man who dominates her so completely is hard to say. As a matter of fact, Mr. Smith is younger, more attractive, and better educated than is his wife.

The only indication of change comes from Mrs. Smith's interview: "I think lately I am sticking up for my rights a little more than before."

The only illustration in support of this contention was in telling Mr. Smith that he was too strict with the children. Outside of this incident no observable change has taken place in husband-wife relations. It is true that Mr. Smith is still the family provider as a WPA worker.

It is interesting to speculate concerning the possible effects of prolonged unemployment in a case of this sort. It is not possible to predict the outcome without more knowledge of the character structure of these submissive wives. How much repressed hostility may there be in her apparent meekness? Is there any repressed desire to dominate, or rivalry with her husband? In order to forecast changes in husband-wife relations we must also know more concerning the personality of the husband and his possible behavior in the face of prolonged unemployment.

"Emotional Bondage." In two of our cases the wife's attitude may be best described as "emotional bondage." The wife is deeply in love with an unworthy husband, about whom she complains bitterly and who, she feels, has caused her nothing but suffering.

Mrs. Kilpatrick is socially and culturally superior to her husband. The husband was a sailor who said that the day after his marriage he regretted the step and was unfaithful to his wife two weeks after marriage. He is not the marrying kind. He feels that marriage is a burden to him. During the 18 years of their married life he was a fairly good provider, but would go off now and then on little trips, and in general did pretty much as he pleased. The wife said that during the last 16 years she has been considering the possibility of leaving him, and all of her married life was a cruel conflict between the desire to leave him and the desire to stay. He told the interviewer that his wife was much too good for him, and he didn't deserve her tolerance, but he couldn't help himself. Since unemployment the family has been on relief and assisted by her relatives. Unemployment made the husband more restless than ever, and he spends night after night away from home. Whenever the wife begins to reproach him, he puts on his hat and leaves the house. She reproaches him for not worrying enough about the family's welfare, and not looking for a job hard enough. She can't imagine that he worries, since he goes out so often and probably has a good time. Furthermore, he never tells her whether he is, or is not, looking for a job. She doesn't know what he has done during the day. (The interviewer got the impression that the husband was eager to find work and looked for it fairly energetically.) In spite of these dissatisfactions the wife is ready to forgive her husband at the slightest show of attention. She said that she would like nothing better than to take a walk with him in the evening, or to have him stay and play cards with the family. When he does show a little attention, she is always hopeful that it will mark a turning point in their relations. She gave all kinds of explanations for not leaving him, but finally confessed that she still loved him.

A similar case is found in the story of an unemployed auto-mechanic who was unfaithful to his wife, was mean to the children, was strict with his wife, and restricted her social life. She feels that unemployment is his fault. But, in spite of it all, the wife says that she would be only too glad to continue living with him if he would reform. "A woman can miss a man just because she is used to him." "Somehow," she said, "I could never hold a grudge against him. Maybe I still love him."

We cannot go into the problem of the origin of such attitudes. In the two cases that we have, unemployment did not affect the wife's attitude. It is true that the wives blame the husbands for unemployment, but that blame does not change their relations. These marriages were always characterized by continuous recriminations and blame, together with a readiness to forgive the husband at the slightest opportunity, and that is very much the picture that exists at present.

The following explanation for the absence of change may be suggested. Love for the husband prior to unemployment was not based upon admiration for him. It was something quite apart from his competence as a provider, or other qualities. Since that was the case, further failures in the sphere brought about by unemployment were simply irrelevant to the wife's feelings. He was deceiving and neglecting her prior to unemployment, and she loved him. Additional failures did not make any difference.

4

PERSONALITY CHANGES OF THE UNEMPLOYED HUSBAND

AND HIS STATUS

THE fate of the husband's authority is to some extent in his own hands. His own behavior during unemployment is a factor in the loss or preservation of his authority. Economic privations, loss of the provider role, loss of daily work routine are all aspects of unemployment which may affect the personality and the behavior of the individual.

A considerable proportion of the men exhibited a certain deterioration of personality: loss of emotional stability, breakdown of morale, irritability, new faults such as drinking, unfaithfulness to the wife, and so on.

Improvement in the man's personality was a much less frequent reaction to unemployment, but it did occur. The man became more thoughtful towards members of the family, more helpful, less irritable. In a few cases the improvement was less directly related to the man's behavior toward the family. Thus, for example, one man became religious. His deeply religious wife rejoiced over the conversion of her husband. Even if this conversion had not made for improvement in the husband's attitude towards her, she would have been compensated by it for any hardships his unemployment may have brought about.

It is often impossible to say which of these changes constituted a deliberate attempt on the part of the man to preserve his status in the face of danger and which, on the other hand, were reactions to other forces. Sometimes the improvement in the man is apparently consciously motivated by the desire to preserve the love of the family, if not his status. It is as if the man hopes, by offering more of his personality, to compensate the family for the loss of his earnings. The man who said, "I try to control my irritability so that the children will not get disgusted with me," and who, according to the testimony of the children, used to be more irritable prior to unemployment, is a case in point. The same process may take place even when it is not verbalized by the man.

In other cases it does not appear that the beneficial changes in the man are motivated by the anxiety for his status. It seems, rather, that he feels deeply the privations of the family and tries to lighten their life out of sympathy for them.

As an illustration of the improvement in the man, take the following testimony:

Mrs. Lake said, "Since unemployment my husband does more for us than ever. He tries hard to make the children love him, and make me feel more towards him. He simply cannot do enough for us. I know that he tries, and I don't know why he should. He knows that we all love him." The wife feels that he is an ideal husband, even if he is out of work. He always does what she asks him to do—plays with the children when they are cranky, and tries to amuse them. The man is very much perturbed about the needs of the family, but attempts to control his worry and irritability, and has become more tender to the family.

Mrs. Brown noted that since unemployment she has become nervous and has had spells of irritation, but her husband has been more patient with her than ever. He has done his "darndest" to get the family out of the depression. Whenever she has had the blues, he has encouraged her and told her how loyal she has been and how much he appreciates her cooperation. He told her that she was an understanding woman and much better than most wives. He has been more attentive to her than he used to be.

A third group of men did not exhibit either favorable or unfavorable changes. These men might have experienced anxiety because of unemployment, but this did not bring about any striking changes in them. It does not mean that in all cases classified under "no change" the man was energetic and resourceful in his search for work. Such cases were included under "no change," but others in the group consisted of men who, prior to unemployment, may not have been ambitious or self-controlled, but who merely did not change during unemployment.

THE HUSBAND'S BEHAVIOR DURING UNEMPLOYMENT AS A FACTOR
IN HIS STATUS

Out of 57 cases which yielded information concerning the
man's behavior, deterioration in the man's personality was observed in 22 cases, "no change" in 24 cases, and improvement
in 11 cases.

Table 4 presents the correlation between the man's behavior
and the effect of unemployment upon his authority:

TABLE 4

THE HUSBAND'S BEHAVIOR AND THE EFFECT OF UNEMPLOYMENT

Husband's Behavior	Husband's Authority		
	Loss	No Loss	Total
Deterioration [9].......	7	15	22
No change...........	4	20	24
Improvement........	2	9	11
Unknown...........	—	—	2
Totals..........	13	44	59

The behavior of the husband does apparently play a role in
the loss or preservation of his status. The husband who changes
for the worse stands a somewhat greater risk of losing status
than the one who does not, and is much less secure than the one
who improves his behavior towards the family.

Table 4 may be interpreted in various ways. The behavior of
the man may be considered as a cause of loss or preservation
of his authority.

It may be, however, that some other factor is a cause both of
changes in the man and of the effects of unemployment upon
his authority. Instrumental attitudes of the wife may be such

[9] It may be questioned whether it was possible to distinguish between the
reaction of the man to unemployment and his reaction to deterioration
of authority. It may be argued that the deterioration of the man's personality in the 7 loss cases may be the result rather than the cause of loss
of authority. An attempt was made to distinguish on the basis of all the
evidence contained in the case between the behavior of the man in the
early days of unemployment and his reaction to the loss of his status.
(See pp. 40-41.)

a factor. It may be that instrumental attitudes result in objectionable changes in the man because he may realize that his status is threatened by unemployment. Instrumental attitudes of the wife were also found to lead to loss of authority. Thus the association between unfavorable changes in the man and loss of authority may be due, not to the direct effect of the man's behavior, but to instrumental attitudes.

Again, it may be that the same personality weaknesses that led to negative changes in the man also led to instrumental attitudes. In such a situation there may be no causal relation between instrumental attitudes and negative changes. The association between the two may be due to their relation to a third factor—weakness in the man—and the loss of authority may be the immediate result of instrumental attitudes.

Some light may be thrown on these alternative explanations by the following table which reveals the association between grounds of authority and the man's behavior:

TABLE 5

Wife's Attitude	Husband's Personality			
	Deterioration	No Change	Improvement	Total
Instrumental......	5	4	2	11
Mixed...........	6	4	1	11
Primary..........	12	15	8	35
Totals........	23	23	11	57

Table 5 shows some correlation between grounds of authority and behavior of the man. The most striking differences appear when instrumental and mixed grounds combined are compared with the primary. Out of 22 instrumental and mixed cases, 11 show deterioration in the man and 3 show improvement. Out of 35 primary cases, 12 show deterioration and 8 show improvement. Inasmuch as the correlation between grounds and behavior of the man is not complete, it can be assumed that the behavior of the man is a factor in the loss or preservation of his authority.

A more complete interpretation of the effect of unemployment upon the husband's status is obtained when his behavior is considered jointly with the attitude of the wife. In Table 6 we have divided the families according to the attitude of the wife and the behavior of the husband on the one hand, and the effect of unemployment on the other.

TABLE 6

THE WIFE'S ATTITUDE, HUSBAND'S BEHAVIOR AND THE EFFECT OF
UNEMPLOYMENT

Wife's Attitude	Loss	No Loss
Primary, with no deterioration in husband.............	1	22
Primary, with deterioration in husband................	1	11
Mixed, with no deterioration in husband..............	0	5
Mixed, with deterioration in husband.................	3	3
Instrumental, with no deterioration in husband........	3	3
Instrumental, with deterioration in husband...........	5	0
Total...	13	44

Apparently, the fate of the unemployed husband's authority
depends largely upon two factors—the predepression attitude of
the wife and his own behavior during unemployment. In the
bulk of our cases the loss or preservation of the husband's
authority may be explained completely in terms of these two
factors.[10]

Primary authority is the surest safeguard the husband has
against loss of authority. Whatever the pattern of dominance
prior to unemployment, whatever his behavior during unemployment, his status is secure. Only two out of 35 cases show loss.

If the grounds are mixed, he will also be secure, provided his
behavior does not deteriorate. But even if his personality does
change for the worse, he still has an equal chance of maintaining
his authority, depending on other factors not taken into account
by the table.

When the grounds are instrumental, the husband wages on
the whole a losing battle. If his behavior deteriorates, there is
no chance of preserving his status, but even if there are no
changes in his personality, he still runs the risk of losing it.[11]

The following cases illustrate the interrelation between attitudes of the wife and changes in the husband. Some show how
primary attitudes of the wife offset objectionable changes in the
husband's personality. The others illustrate the fact that beneficial changes in the man may be of no avail when the attitude
of the wife is instrumental.

One unemployed hatter has shown very little enterprise in
looking for work. His wife, however, became so discouraged by
the depression and so personally dependent upon the husband

[10] This result is valid only within the limits of our sample. It may well
be that a different sample would show exceptions to this generalization.

[11] The last group was divided with regard to the relative status of the
husband prior to unemployment.

that she is glad when he decides to stay at home and not go out in search of work. She says that she feels braver when he is around. Active search for work means his absence from home. *The discouragement of the wife and her personal dependence upon the husband created psychological compensations for his lack of energy.*

In another family, certain objectionable changes in the husband did not lead to any loss of authority. In this case the husband is despondent and broken by unemployment. He refuses to go to the relief office, shifts the burden of the children's discipline to his wife. The wife might have felt some resentment toward her husband for these changes, but she is afraid that he might commit suicide as his brother did, and because of this she spares him unnecessary worries and encourages him. *The effect of discouragement and broken morale of the husband was thus offset by the devotion of the wife.*

In two families, the continued insistence of the husband upon his claim as the head of the family tended to preserve his status. The wife was brought up in a patriarchal tradition and expected her husband to play the role of head of the family. His refusal to make any concessions operated as a deterrent of loss. Needless to say, the husband's inflexibility is a deterrent only under certain conditions. It presupposes a certain amount of admiration for the husband, devotion to him, and the acceptance of the patriarchal pattern. With different attitudes the failure of the husband to modify his claims may be a factor in the loss of his authority. *But at least in two families the inflexibility of the husband and his refusal to make any concessions deterred loss of*

TABLE 7

Instrumental—No Deterioration of Behavior	Loss	No Loss
Woman dominant	2	0
Man dominant	0	2
Balance of power	1	1
Total	3	3

The table suggests that the greater the power of the man prior to unemployment the more chance of preserving his authority. If he was the dominant spouse prior to unemployment and his behavior does not deteriorate, he keeps his status. If the wife was dominant he loses it. If he had equal power with his wife he has an equal chance of maintaining his authority.

authority because it was in line with the patriarchal upbringing of the wife.

In still another family the wife was the more aggressive of the two spouses. She said, "My husband doesn't have any push, but I like him that way." She apparently liked to play the psychological role of a mother and forgave her husband his lack of ambition. *In this case the maternal feeling of the wife offset the influence of the husband's lack of initiative and drive.*

In the two following families *beneficial changes in the husband were of no avail because of instrumental attitudes of the wives:*

Mr. Baldwin became more thoughtful, kinder, more helpful with the housework, but the wife's attitude was so antagonistic that his attempts were of no avail. He undertook a large share of household duties to relieve his wife, but she only said, "If you were employed, you could hire a maid to do it."

Mr. Kilpatrick did not take his unemployment tragically, although he was quite aggressive in his search for a job. His self-possessed attitude and absence of anxiety, however, merely irritated his wife because they seemed to her but another indication of his indifference to her and the family.

The husband's status was preserved in a few cases apparently because the wife felt that despite his failure as a provider she was still her husband's debtor. Husband-wife relations involve some more or less conscious accounting of mutual claims and liabilities. In some cases, circumstances taking place since the husband's loss of employment reduced the wife's contributions and therefore her claims. In one family, for example, the wife became an invalid. Her invalidism put a great strain upon the family. She was completely helpless and dependent upon her husband to attend to all of her needs. Her sickness handicapped her husband in his search for work. She confessed that she could ill afford to blame her husband for his irritability when she was such a burden to him.

It is interesting to note here again that the *loss of claims on the part of the wife served as a deterrent only when her attitude was primary or mixed.* When her attitude was instrumental, the wife discovered some grounds for blame. If her sickness proved a burden to the family, she would say that had it not been for poverty and anxiety, had she been able to obtain better medical care, her sickness might have been prevented.

This modifying effect of the wife's attitude applies also to the problem of blame for unemployment. The wife with primary attitudes tended to absolve her husband from blame whether or not there existed factors mitigating his responsibility for unemployment. Where the attitude was instrumental, the wife tended to blame the husband even if his responsibility for unemployment was slight. Such a wife might blame the husband for lack of education, for marrying too young or too old, for being too aggressive or not aggressive enough, for failure to take a certain step in some remote past.

It is when the attitude of the wife is mixed that his responsibility for unemployment seems to play a role. The responsibility is gauged by the relative spread of unemployment in the husband's trade. In general, the more obvious the extent of unemployment in a particular trade, the less likely is the wife to blame the husband for unemployment. If a whole industrial plant was shut, if stoppage of activity in the husband's trade was an obvious one, as in the building trades, if the wife knew of many others in the same line of work who were idle, she was less likely to hold the husband responsible for unemployment. If, on the other hand, the husband was one of only a few of the salesmen of some large company who have been laid off, there may be some question as to his responsibility. The same may be true in case the husband worked in the manufacture of producers' goods, slackness in which was not obvious to the community. Unemployed husbands testify to more reproaches for unemployment in the early days of the depression before unemployment became general.

What Determines the Man's Reaction to Unemployment?

The man's reaction to unemployment was shown to be one of the factors in the fate of his authority. It would be important to go back of his reaction to unemployment and inquire into conditions that determined it. The problem bears largely upon the structure of the man's personality. No personality tests were given in the course of the study, and therefore no attempt was made at statistical treatment of personality factors. Instead, a few general observations will be offered on two or three aspects of personality which appear to bear upon the problem.[12]

---

[12] While there exist fairly reliable personality tests with regard to some traits, they were not employed in this study. Some tests which refer to the relatively stable traits, as, for example, the intelligence test, might have been employed to advantage, but since it is the predepression personality that we are concerned with in our search for conditioning factors, it is doubtful that personality tests given at the time of our interview would have been warranted.

Individuals vary in their reactions to hardships. Some become disorganized by hardships more easily than others. They become more panicky in the face of hardship. Various personality traits undoubtedly converge to give a person this or that attitude to crises: a relative sense of security in general, a relative amount of resources in other spheres which might compensate for the hardships, a relative placidity of temperament, and so on.

We can narrow down the search for personality traits which account for the man's reaction to unemployment by analyzing what unemployment must mean to the man. Unemployment brings at least three changes into the life of the unemployed man in addition to economic need: (1) loss of the provider role in the family, (2) economic failure with its prestige implications, and (3) loss of daily work routine. What, in the personality of the man, will determine how much these changes disturb his equilibrium and therefore affect his behavior during unemployment? The considerations center about the following problems: The extent to which work was the means of self-expression for the man, and the extent to which his self-esteem was identified with his socio-economic status or his role of the family provider. It is to these problems that we now turn.

The Role of the Family Provider and the Self-Esteem of the Man. It is the man's duty to provide for the family. This pattern is apparently taken for granted by the cultural group to which our families belong. What does this role as a provider mean to the man? Does his self-esteem rest upon it? Does being the provider appear to him the core of his role in the family, the foundation upon which rests his claims to authority and respect? And, conversely, does loss of employment mean a profound sense of failure? Does it arouse fear for his status in the family?

The general impression that the interviews make is that in addition to sheer economic anxiety the man suffers from deep humiliation. He experiences a sense of deep frustration because in his own estimation he fails to fulfill what is the central duty of his life, the very touchstone of his manhood—the role of family provider. The man appears bewildered and humiliated. It is as if the ground had gone out from under his feet. He must have derived a profound sense of stability from having the family dependent upon him. Whether he had considerable authority within the family and was recognized as its head, or whether the wife's stronger personality had dominated the family, he nevertheless derived strength from his role as a provider. Every purchase of the family—the radio, his wife's new hat, the children's skates, the meals set before him—all were symbols of their dependence upon him. Unemployment changed it all. It is to the relief office, or to a relative, that the family now turns. It is to an uncle or a neighbor that the children now turn in expectation of a dime or a nickel for ice cream, or the larger beneficences such as a bicycle or an excursion to the amusement park.[13]

The feeling of disturbance and humiliation apparently exists irrespective of the intellectual convictions of the man. The men show different and almost contradictory verbal reactions to the situation. There are some who say, "If a child is well brought up, he will certainly not lose respect for his father just because his father happens to be out of work." Or, "Perhaps in foreign-born families children do lose respect for their unemployed fathers. It will not happen in any well-brought-up American

[13] Underlying the seriousness with which the man views his role as a provider is his general acceptance of the institution of the family and his responsibility for it. To the majority of the men the family was an unquestioned part of their lives. Not all of the men, of course, were competent providers prior to the depression. Some were shiftless and others drank heavily, but even these, however they may have rationalized their behavior in hot arguments with the wife or relatives, had a sense of guilt towards the family.

Only a very few of the men wished they had never married. Mr. Jones said that if he had it all to do over again he would not marry. His idea of an ideal life was to knock around from one country to another, constantly seeking new fortunes and new adventures. Marriage tied him down. Mr. Kilpatrick said that he realized too late that he was not a family man. But he, incidentally, regrets his marriage, not because of the responsibilities it thrust upon him, but because he feels he was unfair to his wife and children and he considers it *his* defect that he cannot be faithful to one woman for a long time.

The majority, however, expressed no regrets concerning marriage, although in several cases they wished they had married different persons. Again and again both men and women wished they had not had so many children.

It doesn't mean, of course, that family life was a refuge and a blessing to the majority of the men. It may have been a burden, but if it was, it was so unquestioned and accepted a burden that the alternative of a single life did not exist in the consciousness. The answer to the question of what the man would do with one thousand dollars was quite revealing. Very few men said they would use the money to liberate themselves from the family. Those few said that they would first provide for the family and then go away and live independently—doing as they pleased and forgetting family troubles. But the majority of the men would spend the one thousand dollars within the family—establish a business, fix up the furniture, send the children to school, and so on.

family." Or, "A wife who would desert her husband just because he is unemployed is not worth a d——." Or, "I would break the children's necks if there was any hint of disrespect."

On the other hand, there were some who said, "It's only natural that the unemployed father should lose authority with the children." "Children's love must be bought." "Children love parents in gratitude for things that the parents do for them." "It's inevitable that the children will begin to wonder why their old man can't get a job." "It is the father's job to provide for the family. The children can't help but resent it if he fails in his duty."

But whether the men said that it was natural or immoral and subversive for an unemployed man to lose status within the family, they felt equally disturbed by ·their plight.

The best way to describe the sense of uselessness and the anxiety of the men, their pathetic grasp at what little remains of their role as providers, is to let the men speak for themselves.

Profound, indeed, must be the importance of the role of the provider for the man's self-esteem to cause him to say, "I would rather starve than let my wife work." Or, "I would rather turn on the gas and put an end to the whole family than let my wife support me."

One man said that the worst thing about unemployment was having to go on relief. The next worst thing was having his wife work, as she had for a few months. To be supported by her, even for a short time, made him very unhappy. In fact, he is sure they would have drifted apart if she had continued longer. He would have left her. The whole thing was wrong. She was not the same; he was not the same. It was awful to have to ask her for tobacco, or to have to tell the landlady, "My wife will come, and I will pay you," or to be expected to have the dinner ready when she came home, or to have her too tired to talk to him at dinner. When he works and comes home tired, she is waiting for him and they have a nice talk together. But the other way it was quite different. At one time both of them worked. That was better. Then the one who got home first cooked the meal. But even that was all wrong.

It is interesting to see that in this particular family the wife is devoted to the husband and has attempted to make her employment as painless as possible for her husband. She tells this story:

When she first told her husband that she would look for work, he disapproved of it. She went right ahead. She could tell that every evening he was anxious until she told him that the search for work during the day had been fruitless. He could hardly conceal his pleasure. One day she did find a job in a department store. His first reaction was to tell her that in times of depression it is easier for a woman to find a job than it is for a man. She knew that he was unhappy and sulky, and tried to think of some way of reconciling him to her work. At the end of the first week she asked him to come to the store and meet some people she worked with, and also to help her carry the pay envelope home. He said he wouldn't come, but at closing time she found him waiting for her. After a while she noticed that he hated to have her pay the rent. She decided to let him pay the rent. Her sudden sickness made her discontinue working. She doesn't think he would have become reconciled to it had she continued for a long time.

One unemployed painter has a fine face which is lined with anxiety. He is 40 years old, but looks years older. He still has a position of authority in the family, but this doesn't allay his suffering. He feels that a father who is not a provider cannot possibly keep the love of the children. It was pathetic and significant to hear him repeat several times in the course of the interview that it was he who still provided the family with shelter and "kept the roof over their heads." "And isn't this, after all, the most important thing?" he appealed anxiously to the interviewer. He earned $25 a month as janitor of a church, and this money went for the rent of the family.

Not every man described his feelings so frankly and directly. There were many of the men who showed their anxieties only indirectly. One father, for example, forbade his children to play with other children of the neighborhood so that they would not make too many comparisons between him and the employed fathers of their friends. Another asked his wife at various intervals whether or not his children had said anything about his unemployment. One husband said that sex contacts with his wife were reduced on his initiative, while it is certain that it was his wife who insisted upon it.

While the above quotations express the dominant reaction, there was a group which apparently did not experience this humiliation and fear of loss of status. A few in this group were always so irresponsible and indifferent to the family that unemployment did not affect them. There was another small number of men however, who, felt deeply their inability to support the family, but nevertheless were not broken by it. It seems as if their dominant sentiment is economic anxiety rather than humiliation. They feel that unemployment is not their fault and give no indication of humiliation or fear for their status.

We see, thus, that the men vary in their reaction to the loss of the role of family provider. It is apparently more strongly tied up with the self-esteem of some men than of others. The explanation is a difficult problem. Perhaps it lies in part in the relative strength of patriarchal mores in the upbringing of the man, in part in the relative security that the man feels in personal relations within his family.

In so far as these factors make unemployment a particularly strong shock to some men and not to others, they also affect the behavior of the men during unemployment and hence the destiny of their authority.

Economic Failure and the Self-Esteem of the Man: Economic failure of the man was considered in the preceding pages in its relation to the husband's role in the family, but it has other aspects. It brings about retrenchments in the standard of living and loss of social status. One of the main grounds for prestige in our society is success in the economic sphere. To be defeated in the economic world is a failure which implies loss of social status.

All of the men in our families gave one or another indication of accepting the above valuations and of worrying over the loss of social status. Some admitted it, others revealed it indirectly. (See the section on "Social Life of the Unemployed.")

While most of the unemployed men felt some loss of status and experienced some anxiety over it, they varied in the intensity of their reaction. This is illustrated by the Page and the Scott families.

Mr. Page was a truck driver. He said he was never particular about the kind of a job he had; he preferred not to work so hard and to have time to spend with his family. His wife encouraged him in this attitude. They were satisfied with their standard of living because their tastes were simple. His wife never cared to spend money on clothes. In fact, he always had to urge her to get a new dress. They didn't care for the good times that cost a lot of money. They both were homebodies and liked nothing better than to spend an evening at home with their children or with friends. The friends that they had were their own kind and came to see them even though they didn't spend lots of money on entertaining. Mr. Page was a good bridge player and was always in demand for a game in the neighborhood.

Since loss of employment the husband shares all the household activities with his wife. In spite of the hardships of the depression the wife is highly pleased with her husband. He is helpful in the house, devoted to her, cheerful, and a great help with the children. Of course she wants him to get a job, but she hates to think of losing his companionship during the day. Their social life has not been affected by the depression. Mrs. Page told their friends not to invite them to their homes because she no longer could return their invitations, but their friends come to visit them as often as before. They frequently bring their own refreshments with them. "Take last night, for example," said Mrs. Page. "Some friends came over and played games and had a very good time. Better, in fact, than they might have had if I had arranged a party, worked all day before and after the party, and spent a lot of money on it."

In contrast to the Page's, take the Scott family. At the time of marriage the wife said that she and her husband had hopes of conquering the world together. The husband was to save money and go into business for himself. She was very much satisfied with her husband prior to unemployment because he was more ambitious than many of their friends and was always striving for a better position in society. She had always something to look forward to. She was confident that as the years went by she could afford more things and improve their standard of living and their associations. "A good husband is the kind who has the zeal to elevate himself both economically and socially."

Unemployment was a great blow to both the husband and the wife. The wife said that the economic failure of her husband was a bitter disappointment to her. She thought he was the kind of a man who had enough ability to make good. She now sees that she was mistaken.

Mr. Scott confessed that he lost his self-respect because of his unemployment. The social life of the couple has been broken up. The husband has no money to maintain his club affiliations. They have broken all relations with friends at the insistence of the husband, because they have no clothes to wear and no money to entertain with. The only visitor to the house is an old bachelor friend of the husband.

Mr. Scott's relations with his children have deteriorated. Both husband and wife think that it is natural that children should lose respect for a father who cannot provide for them.

Even these partial glimpses of the two families suggest sharp differences in their life goals. The aspirations of the Scott family centered about its economic and social improvement— to have a better home, to dress better, to entertain well. In other words, to pass into the next higher economic and prestige scale of living. The Page family, on the other hand, is almost completely outside this competitive game. It seems that this is the result, not of a withdrawal from economic competition out of fear, but is rather due to positive satisfactions that the family finds in other spheres. Instead of increasing the earning ability and enabling the family to live better, dress better, meet with "nicer" people, the Page couple preferred a job that would give the husband more leisure with the family. The family is, of course, anxious concerning economic needs, but that is because the relief money does not allow even a minimum of adequate food, clothing, and medical care.

Many factors have to be taken into consideration to account for the differences in the life goals of individual families. While the dominant values of our culture lay great stress on economic prowess, our society is so differentiated that various groups within it (and various individuals within the groups) may have a somewhat different hierarchy of values. However, since most of the families come from the same cultural and socio-economic group, the differences are probably due to personality configurations rather than any variations in the cultural heritage. The whole life history of the family would have to be understood to explain what it is that made both Mr. and Mrs. Page more self-sufficient and less dependent upon social recognition, more satisfied with cultivation of personal relations within the family, possessing tastes that do not require much money for their satisfaction, and so on. But whatever explains it, it is clear that the men in the two families must react to unemployment in a different fashion. Mr. Scott built his life upon the materialistic values, depending for his security upon maintaining the customary social status, measuring his worth in terms of economic success. The economic failure was not so great a shock for Mr. Page.

The Daily Work Routine as a Means of Expression for the Man. "I am going crazy with so much time on my hands and nothing to do." Such was the most usual reaction to the loss of daily routine. There was not a single man among the 59 who welcomed freedom from the lifelong routine of work, to whom this freedom was a compensation, however slight, for the curse of unemployment. It is clear, of course, that the leisure of the unemployed is so filled with economic privations, anxiety, and humiliation, that it is quite different from the leisure of the employed man. However, quite apart from economic privations, the unemployed man suffered from loss of daily routine.

There is generally every reason to expect dislocation of life as a result of loss of work. Most of the men in our cases are middle-aged men whose lives for many years have been organized around their daily work, and the sheer habit would make for a feeling of loss at sudden unemployment.

Furthermore, for most of the men in our culture, work is apparently the sole organizing principle and the only means of self-expression. The other interests that existed in the lives of these men—active sports, hobbies, political and civic interests, personal and social relations—turned out to be too weak and insignificant for their personalities to furnish any meaning to their lives. Work, the chief, and in many cases only, outlet was closed to the men, and they faced complete emptiness.

There are several factors which make it difficult for unemployed men to pursue even such hobbies as they may have had, or to develop new interests. Many men testify that their acute anxiety concerning the welfare of their families is so demoralizing that they cannot concentrate even on their usual hobbies and activities. Several remarked that the busier they were the more they got done, and complained about having too much time. Apparently, the very formlessness of the day and the week, the absence of any required tasks, caused a letdown and weakened the drive for any activity. This reaction is typical of the unemployed and is part of the generally paralyzing effect of unemployment which has been noted in several studies.

Even those men who do have hobbies get no satisfaction from their pursuit of them. They feel that hobbies are trivial and undignified when they form the main content of life. This derives, in part, from the dominant philosophy of life which glorifies work.

The average American has the feeling that work—activities connected with making a living—is the only dignified way of life; that no man worthy of his name would be satisfied with growing flowers or painting pictures as the main activity of life unless, indeed, he intended to sell them. While theoretically, economic activities are supposed to be the means to the good life, as a matter of fact it is not the end, but the means themselves, that have the greater prestige. The cultivation of ends for their own sake—playing the violin, reading, engaging in artistic hobbies—is all very well if it is a supplement to a busy, productive life in the economic world. The young, or even the middle-aged man, who made these things the center of his life would be held in some contempt even if he had an independent income.

While most men share the above reactions, there are some interesting personality differences. This is manifested, for example, in different answers to the question: "Is time heavy on your hands?" The majority answered: "I am going crazy with nothing to do. I would take some work just to be doing something, even if there was no money in it." To the question, "What hit you hardest about unemployment?" these individuals mention idleness side by side with economic worries. Still a third characteristic reaction distinguishes this group. To the question, "What is the most important thing in life?" they are likely to say, "Work, because with nothing to do you cannot enjoy anything."

But there were a few who in answer to the question "Is time heavy on your hands?" said "No, I manage to keep myself busy." They did not mention idleness as an important problem of unemployment, and to the question, "What is the most important thing in life?" might mention health or happiness, or family life. When they mentioned work, it was only as a guarantee of financial security.

Personality traits which make the disruption of the daily work routine a particularly strong shock to some men, rather than to others, also affect their behavior during unemployment and hence the destiny of their authority.

Such are the general considerations concerning the personality of the man which lie behind his reaction to unemployment. We have seen that many different attitudes probably converge to determine this reaction. What cultural patterns formed the man's outlook on family life? How deeply rooted were these patterns? What were the life goals or ego ideals of the man—how much tied up with the maintenance of his socio-economic status? What resources did the man have in addition to the skills involved in making a living? How secure was he personally? And so on.

It is obvious, of course, that the personality of the husband

and his relation with the wife are not isolated and independent factors. They are aspects of a continuous interacting whole. One thing that might make a person easygoing, for example, is his happy adjustment in the family, and on the other hand, his personality may make for better marital adjustments. The attitudes of the wife, the behavior of the wife at the beginning of unemployment, constitute in themselves factors affecting the reaction of the man. By considering separately the behavior of the man we do not intend to deny the obvious fact that his behavior is in part a result and in part a determinant of the authoritarian relation.

5

THE UNEMPLOYED FATHER

AND THE YOUNG CHILD

AN unemployed truck driver expressed what is the prevailing belief among our families as to the role of the father in the family. "It is the mother's place to bring up the children and the father's place to provide for them. It is natural for the mother to be closer to the children, but for the father to have greater control over them." The physical care of the children was invariably considered the mother's special province but her duties were felt to extend also to most other aspects of daily routine, helping children with homework, contacts with the school, supervision of their recreation, and general discipline. While the mother was thus considered to be the chief agent in the daily care and education of the children, the father's role was conceived as that of a more aloof but also more respected and feared parent, the court of last resort. The father's authority was, as it were, kept in reserve for problems with which the mother could not cope herself.

One father put it this way: "Now that I am at home all day I get irritated with the children, and they feel that I have become a nag. When I used to work I would ask my wife in the evening, 'Were Johnny and Willie good boys today?' and then I would either punish or reward them. And that's how it should be."

Another belief held by the parents was that a father must take a greater interest in the boy and the mother in the girl. Furthermore, that while the mother is concerned with the young children up to 14 or 15, when the child begins to face the really serious problems of life he must turn to his father. Such were the professed beliefs. However, only about one-half of the cases conformed to this stereotype of the mother as the chief agent in supervising daily activities and the father as the more aloof but more respected and feared parent. In 15 families out of 59 the pattern of the family relations bore very little resemblance to this stereotype. The mother was forceful and dominant and the father the more lenient parent of the two. In these families it was the father who interceded for the children and the mother provided what is usually considered the masculine role. It was against the mother's will that the child must oppose his own. The struggle for emancipation, if there was such, was from the mother's authority. The mother was the taskmaster and the censor of activities and identified with the duty principle. It was her commands and standards that might have become internalized in the child's own conscience. It was to the father that the child turned for unconditional affection not dependent upon his being "good" or "bad."

In a few cases, the roles of father and mother were not differentiated, and still others deviated from the stereotype in that the father not only had the superior authority but was also the chief agent in supervising daily activities of the children.

It is interesting to observe what happens in families which differ most from the professed pattern. Does the discrepancy cause difficulties? It is revealing that only 4 men in the 15 families in which the mother dominated the children admitted that their wives had greater control over the children. One way apparently of facing the discrepancy between the stereotype and reality is to deny it. Other fathers in this group rationalized the mother's superior control as her greater intimacy with the children. "It is only natural that the children should be closer to their mother." The men were lucky if the children in question happened to be girls. Then they would say, "If we had boys I would be closer to them, but you would expect the girls to be closer to their mother." Another rationalization was in projecting the blame upon the wife. One father said that he disapproved of the wife's strictness. He described his helplessness with the children as a deliberate educational policy of leniency.

In still other cases, the father presented the situation as a result of his deliberate choice. He said that he withdrew from disciplining the children because of disagreements between himself and his wife. He decided that it was bad for the children to have two rulers.

When husband-wife relations were strained and the wife dominated the children, the husband accused the wife of "poisoning the children" against him.

We turn now to the effect of unemployment upon the status of the father. What happens to his authority when he becomes unemployed?

THE FREQUENCY OF CHANGES

We shall first present the results of the study with regard to the general frequency of changes in the following table:

TABLE 8

EXTENT OF CHANGE IN THE FATHER'S AUTHORITY
ALL CHILDREN 7 YEARS OLD AND OVER

	Boys	Girls	Total	Total in Per Cent
No change...	57	58	115	75
Gain........	6	5	11	7
Loss........	13	14	27	18
Totals....	76	77	153	100

Unemployment, as it appears from the table, has not had a uniformly negative effect upon parent-child relations. While the father's authority more often suffers as a result of unemployment, some improvement was observed in a few families. The strengthening of the father's authority, however, was never due to the economic aspects of unemployment. It was the increased presence of the father at home and the possibility of more intimate contact with the children that improved father-child relations.

The extent of loss is identical for boys and girls. Striking differences in the extent of change appear when children of various ages are compared. Table 9 presents the extent of change by ages of children.

The unemployed father is relatively safe with the young child. It is his relation with his adolescent child that is threatened by unemployment. Every successive age group shows an increasingly greater rate of deterioration.

Furthermore, the improvement of the father's authority is limited to the younger children. It occurs only with children under 15 years of age.

TABLE 9

EXTENT OF CHANGE IN THE FATHER'S AUTHORITY BY
AGES OF CHILDREN

Record of All Children

	Years			Total
	7–11	12–14	15 and Over	
No change...	39	30	46	115
Gain........	8	3	—	11
Loss........	3	7	17	27
Totals....	50	40	63	153

That the significance of the father's unemployment should vary with the age of the child is reasonable in the light of the psychology of parent-child relations. The authority of the father is accepted uncritically by the young child. The child is born into a culture that demands obedience to the father. Religion, morals, family rituals, the child's own conscience, all furnish sanctions to the father's authority. The younger the child, the more completely does he accept the traditional attitude that the father must be obeyed. Furthermore, the young child feels helpless against the father. Growing irritability and unreasonableness of the father may be accepted by the young child as an act of nature about which he can do nothing.

The young child is less likely to comprehend the full significance of unemployment. We found that even very young children apparently accept the prestige folkways of our society and feel deeply the shame of poverty and relief. They also feel the economic privations of the family. Nevertheless, the father's unemployment does not disturb their lives to the extent that it does the lives of the older children. Their needs are fewer. Their horizon is more circumscribed by the family, and they are less sensitive to the family's loss of social prestige. The father's personality and behavior within the home mean more to them than his place in the social hierarchy.

The relation of the older child to the father differs in many important respects. The unquestioned acceptance of the father's authority weakens with the age of the child. As a child becomes older, more critical, more independent, paternal authority must be increasingly based upon the personal leadership of the father rather than the power of his office. The older child is less likely to tolerate increasing irritability or other objectionable changes in the father resulting from unemployment. Indeed, adolescence is, even under normal conditions, likely to put a particular strain upon father-child relations. It is a period in which the adolescent frequently struggles for emancipation from paternal authority. The adolescent girl may want to stay out later, wear silk stockings, leave school; the adolescent boy wants to keep a larger share of his earnings, to be free with regard to his associates. With these interests comes a more conscious struggle for self-assertion. From the point of view of the father, the period brings a threat to his power. He often experiences a conflict which adds to the confusion of parent-child relations. The conflict is between his desire to keep the child under his control, or protect the child, on the one hand, and on the other, the desire for responsibility and maturity on the part of the child.

Not only is the older child predisposed to be more critical of any possible changes in the father, but he is likely to react more strongly to other aspects of unemployment. The older child feels the depression keenly. His frustrations may cause resentment against the father and create conflict with the parents. He certainly is more likely to realize the failure on the part of the father implied in the loss of a job.[14]

It is interesting to compare husband-wife and paternal authority relations from the point of view of their susceptibility to unemployment. Table 10 represents the comparative extent of loss of authority.

This table shows that the unemployed man's authority is more precarious with the wife than it is with the younger children, but it is safer with her than it is with the adolescent children. It is his relation with the older children that proves to be the most unstable.

The explanation of the greater stability of the paternal authority in the case of the younger children as compared with

[14] See pp. 140-141 for the problem of discerning the role of unemployment as against other factors in the loss of authority over the adolescent.

TABLE 10

COMPARATIVE EXTENT OF LOSS OF AUTHORITY

	Children Under 12	Children 12 to 14	Wives	Adolescents 15 and Over
Total number of cases.....	50	40	58	63
Number of loss cases......	3 [15]	7	13	17
Per cent of loss cases......	6	18	21	27

the wife may lie in the institutional buttress of the father's authority. The authority of the father is the authority of his office, while the authority of the husband depends to a greater extent upon personal leadership. However much may survive of the patriarchal pattern in marriage, it does not prescribe for the wife anything like the unconditional subordination that our mores prescribe for the child. As a result, the husband has to maintain his authority with his wife through personal leadership, whereas the father can for some years keep his status as an unquestioned consequence of his office as a father.

The greater stability of the husband-wife relations as compared with the father's status with adolescent children also requires an explanation. The man as a person has a different significance for his wife than for his children. If the relations are at all satisfactory, the husband, his companionship, his love, are ends in themselves for the wife. With the older child this is not usually the case. The personal relations with the father play a smaller role. If this is so, then even when the husband is no longer a provider, the wife has more at stake in personal relations with him, and hence shows less change in attitudes.

Because the age of the child proves so significant a determinant of his reaction to the father's unemployment, we shall consider separately the various age groups and discuss first the younger child, the child under 12 years of age.

The unemployed father, as was indicated in the preceding section, does not suffer loss of status with his young child. Out of 50 children between the ages of 7 and 12, only 3 showed deterioration of paternal relations due to unemployment. This fact in itself indicates that it is only under exceptional conditions

[15] Number of families in which one or more than one child changed his attitude towards the father.

that unemployment undermines the authority of the father over a young child. Unless these exceptional conditions exist, the decline of the father's socio-economic status, loss of money as means of control, his constant presence at home, even increased irritability and violence towards the child, do not apparently endanger such authority as the father may have had prior to unemployment.

What are these exceptional configurations which, according to our cases, are strong enough to undermine the father's authority? In the three cases of loss they are strikingly similar: Unemployment has broken the morale of the man so that he himself has relinquished all claims to authority; the child has always been much closer to the mother than to the father, with whom he never had any companionship; husband-wife relations were strained, with the wife openly voicing her dissatisfaction.

Not only was the father's authority over the young children unshaken but some fathers have actually succeeded in turning unemployment into a blessing. In 8 cases the father's authority has been strengthened as a result of unemployment. The analysis of these 8 cases and their comparison with those in which no change has taken place suggests that it is the behavior of the unemployed father and his attitude to the child during the period of unemployment that accounts for the improvement in father-child relations.

IMPROVEMENT IN FATHER-CHILD RELATIONS

The observed strengthening of the father's status sometimes involved a real change in the authoritarian relations. One indulgent, easygoing father changed into a firm and respected parent with a greater control over the children. But more often unemployment has merely intensified the predepression parent-child relations rather than changed their quality. What happened was that the unemployed father took advantage of his increased leisure to extend his contacts with the children and his supervision over more spheres of their lives. Whenever this extended control was accepted by the child without conflict, we considered it as an increase in the father's status.

The increased concern with the children on the part of the father brought about improvement in father-child relations only when such relations were satisfactory prior to unemployment. In every case of gain of status the father had always been an interested father for whom the child had great admiration or, at the very least, affection. Otherwise, the attempt to extend control would only cause conflict or be of no avail.

The attitudes of the children toward the father in such families may be illustrated by the following incidents. When asked whether she would like to have her father go back to work, one 7-year-old girl answered, "It's better both ways. If he worked we would have more money, but if he doesn't work he can play with us." One father says that when the children notice that he is worried, they try to entertain him with stories about school. If there is nothing to tell, he can see that they are making up stories just to keep his mind off his worries. A boy, aged 13, said that whenever he sees that his father is worried, he asks him to criticize his drawings. It is harder, the boy said, to distract his mother from worrying, but father gets interested in showing him how to improve the drawing and forgets his worries at least for a while.

In a few cases the improvement in father-child relations involved a real change in their quality. For example, in one family both parents testified that the father used to be "too easygoing with the children." Being forced since unemployment to share in their daily activities, he was confronted with the serious task of bringing them up and saw the wisdom of his wife's firm educational policies. He acquired better control over the children without any loss of their affection. It was his daughter's words which were quoted above.

Two conditions are apparently necessary to bring about an improvement in father-child relations. In every case of gain in status the father had had particularly satisfactory relations with the children prior to unemployment, and that stood him in good stead during the critical period. Furthermore, he made a special effort to share more fully in the life of the children.

6

THE UNEMPLOYED FATHER

AND THE ADOLESCENT CHILD

THE unemployed father did not fare so well with the adolescent children as with the children under 12. Unemployment has undermined the authority of the father over the adolescent child even more frequently than it has the authority of the husband but for somewhat different reasons.

THE VARIOUS WAYS IN WHICH UNEMPLOYMENT LED TO THE LOSS OF THE FATHER'S AUTHORITY

The increased presence of the man at home strained the man's relation with his children just as it had with his wife. In some cases it led to loss of his status because it brought about increased conflict and a certain disillusionment with him.

"Our Hands Are Tied Without Money." Lack of money, on the other hand, played a somewhat different role in the deterioration of the father's authority. Money was frequently used by the parents as an instrument of education and control, and its loss weakened the father's control in the following ways:

The father could no longer "bribe" his children into obeying orders.

He could no longer withhold things and activities as a means of punishment.

He could not offer good substitutes such as week-end picnics for undesirable activities.

He had to relinquish restrictions in some spheres in compensation for privations in general. "We do not get any fun out of life anyway; at least don't be so strict about hours."

A few citations from the cases will illustrate the way in which loss of money restricted the power of the parent.

Mr. Robinson complained bitterly about complete loss of control over his three boys. They were always out, had no love for their home, came in late, stopped going to church. Mr. Robinson said, "Our hands are tied without money." He looked out of the window and said, pointing to the street, "Now there's one of my boys out there. You see the boy he is playing with? Well, he lies, smokes, drinks, swears, and steals, but what can I do about it? My boy is only 14, and I can't reason much with him. I know that if I had the money, I could think up some ways of inducing him not to play with that boy. For instance, if he had a bicycle, you wouldn't see him around the house five minutes a day. I can give you another illustration. The three oldest children were not permitted to see a movie until they were 16 years old. There was no trouble in enforcing that rule. All we had to say was 'No.' Since the depression I have had to cut five years off the age minimum for movie-going. The children nagged continually, saying that they had to have some fun."

Mr. Robinson said that he could not supply the children with spending money and clothes, and therefore he didn't have the heart to deny them an occasional movie. He felt that rich people had more control over their children than poor people because they could divert them from bad influences by spending money in other directions.

In the family of an unemployed glass worker the major conflict with the boy was over money. The boy resented economic privations. Poverty drove the boy to stealing. The father felt that if he had been able to satisfy the minimum of his son's wants there would have been no problem. By buying things for the boy and giving him a little spending money he thought he could have kept him from his bad associates. Lack of money affected the father's control in still another way. The boy said "It's bad enough that you can't give me money. At least you might let me stay out later and enjoy things that don't cost any money."

Another father said that in addition to his increased presence at home, lack of money had weakened his control over the children. Prior to unemployment, if they misbehaved, he could say, "No movie this week," or, "I would have given you more if you had been a good boy." On the other hand, if they were good during the day it meant nothing for him to give them a nickel or more. The father described the following incident:

His wife had asked their daughter, aged 16, to do some ironing. The girl refused, saying that it was too hot to iron. A friend of the family happened to come in carrying a new yellow pocketbook which the girl admired. The friend said, "If you will iron, I'll get the same kind of a pocketbook for you." Sure enough, his daughter went right to it. If he had been able to promise her gifts he could get her to do anything.

Another way in which unemployment has undermined the father's authority was through its effect on his own personality. The unemployed man has shown greater irritability and over-assertion of power in his relations with his children than with his wife. Owing perhaps to the helplessness of the children, the average unemployed man, restless, distraught, and humiliated, has frequently found it easier to vent his emotions upon his children than upon his wife. Furthermore, the children's behavior offers a particularly sensitive barometer of the man's authority because of the expected obedience. Perhaps, therefore, the father would become aware of threats to his authority sooner and react to them with coercion.

"*Father Is a Changed Man.*" The story of the Cutter family gives a vivid picture of the changes in parental relations due to the effect of unemployment upon the personality of the father.

The Cutter Family

Mr. Cutter	46	Boy	12
Mrs. Cutter	39	Girl	11
Girl	16	Girl	3

Most of the information about the family came from the interview with the girl 16 years old. The interview with the father was practically worthless because he misrepresented the situation. Significantly enough the father refused to allow his children to be interviewed and the interview with the girl took place without his knowledge. The mother was evasive, but confirmed the picture created by the girl's interview.

The girl of sixteen said that her father had changed so much since the depression that she could hardly believe he was the same man. "He used to be so good and kind, and now he is so mean and nasty." The children used to go to him for help in their schoolwork, but in the last year or so he had become so "damned irritable" that if they didn't understand at once, "he hollered to beat the band."

The girl used to be proud of her father—proud to introduce him to her friends. Now she is afraid to bring any friends of hers to her home, not because it isn't nice or decently furnished, but because of what her father might say or do. He might start hitting the children for no good reason at all, or might start an argument with her mother.

Since the depression her father has become very "bossy," and wants his own way in everything. And when he doesn't have his own way he starts an argument. He never used to hit the children before, but now he does so at the slightest provocation. He does not hit the 16-year-old girl "because he knows better." She would run away from home if he hit her. But she cannot keep him from hitting the other children and even her mother. That is what worries her most. About a year and a half ago she first saw him hit her mother, and that has happened several times in the past year. Anything can get him mad. He always tries to start an argument. If, for example, the girl says that she wants to teach English, he will tell her that the English field is all filled and she should study German. But what gets him most are the children's complaints about their needs, not being able to go to a movie, not having clothes, and so on. He tells them he can't help it, that he is sick and unable to find work. But then, should the child keep nagging for a dime, the father beats the child. The last time the father hit her mother was in an argument over his unemployment. Her mother told him to try to get a job with the WPA and he said he was too sick to work. He accused her of wanting him to die. He became very angry and slapped her a couple of times.

The regulation which the girl resents most is her father's refusal to allow her to go out with boys. One day she made a date with a young man in the neighborhood to go to a movie. Her father not only refused to let her go, but when the young man came, her father answered the door himself and told him that his daughter was too young to go out with young men. He didn't even allow her to talk to the young man.

The children mind the father because they are afraid of him. The girl says that she is not afraid of him, but keeps quiet so as not to stir up trouble for her mother and the other children. She feels the depression keenly. She is ashamed to go to school because she has only one childish, shabby dress and coat. She has to wash this dress every two or three days. She might have got some clothes from the E.R.A. but she is afraid that her friends will recognize the source. She conceals the family's plight even from her intimate friends, telling them that her father receives compensation for war injuries. It is hard for her never to be able to go out with her girl friends after school hours. She has to think up all kinds of excuses, but the fact is she never has a nickel or a dime in her pocket. Her girl friends don't understand, and she is afraid she is losing their friendship.

Her father knows how hard the children are hit by the depression. No doubt he is worried about it. Her father often speaks of the money he will get for his war injuries and promises that he will make it up to the family for what they haven't had since the depression. But she thinks that her father could get a job if he weren't always feeling sorry for himself. If he thought less of his ailment and more of his family he could find a job. Besides, no matter how much he worried, she certainly could not forgive him for being so mean and cruel to her mother and the children. In fact, even if he goes back to work and gives her everything she wants, he won't be able to clear himself in her eyes.

Mrs. Cutter was evasive in her interview. She did, however, give some additional information. Prior to the depression her husband was an easygoing, carefree individual who never worried about anything. Since the depression he has become very irritable, "hollers at the children for the least thing" and starts arguments with her. The children obey him "but not because they respect his judgment." They are afraid of him. They complain to her about him. She doesn't speak of it often to her husband because she doesn't want to make him think that "everyone is against him." She believes he became entirely too rough with the children. Mrs. Cutter is convinced that when he goes back to work he will "act himself again."

That the behavior of the unemployed father has led to the loss of his status in some families became apparent through the analysis of the cases. There is, however, additional statistical evidence of the relation between the behavior of the man during unemployment and his authority. Table 11 summarizes this evidence.

The proportion of loss cases is greatest for the men whose behavior has changed for the worse. There are no loss cases among the men who have improved their attitude toward the children.

TABLE 11

THE FATHER'S BEHAVIOR AND THE EFFECT OF UNEMPLOYMENT

Father's Behavior	Father's Authority		
	Loss [16] Families	No-Loss Families	Total Families
Deterioration......	9	13	22
No change.........	7	20	27
Improvement......	—	10	10
Total..........	16	43	59

The Unemployed Father and His Working Child. The Brady case illustrates the relation between the unemployed father and the employed son. The decisive feature in the loss of the father's authority is the failure of the man as a provider, together with the gainful employment of the boy.

The Brady Family

Mr. Brady 46	Boy 22	Girl 15
Mrs. Brady 44	Boy 17	Boy 12
On relief since 1932.		

The boy of seventeen is the only employed member of the family, earning $12 a week.

Mr. Brady is a tall, well-built man with pure white hair combed straight back from a high forehead. He spoke well and concisely in the manner of a man who has arrived at a definite philosophy of life and who wishes to impart it to others.

Mr. Brady was a railroad engineer, earning a good deal of money and living well. He admitted that he used to be unfaithful to his wife. He went out with all kinds of women and drank rather heavily, but his wife was very "sweet" about it, and there were no major conflicts. He always saw to it that she and the children were well provided for. He used to have a violent temper. He left many a job simply because he got into an argument with the boss.

[16] Number of families in which one or more children changed their attitudes towards the father.

Soon after the family went on relief, Mr. Brady got interested in the Pentecost mission, better known by the name of "Holy Rollers." Mrs. Brady has always been very religious. Both of them were "saved" three years ago, and ever since that time they have taken a deep interest in the mission. They attend services, and Mr. Brady is one of the most prominent members of the mission.

Since Mr. Brady's conversion, marital life has been more satisfactory. He doesn't lose his temper as often. Mrs. Brady feels that life with her husband is much happier, and she gives thanks for her husband's salvation. His religious conversion and improvement in his temper apparently fully compensate her for economic hardships. Mr. Brady said, in fact, that his wife's respect for him has grown during the past three years. He has ceased looking for work and spends the day at the mission or reading the Bible or literature on the Bible or talking about politics. He is convinced that Communism, with the exception of its attitude towards the church, is the best political philosophy.

As to the children's reactions to the depression, Mr. Brady says that poorer clothing and being on relief have hit the children hardest. The 15-year-old-girl quit high school because of runs in her stockings, torn shoes, and worn-out dresses that she had to wear.

Mr. Brady says that while the children don't blame him for his unemployment, he is sure that they don't think as much about the old man as they used to. "It's only natural. When a father cannot support his family, supply them with clothing and good food, the children are bound to lose respect." If he had been earning, for example, he would not have allowed his son, 22, to quit school.

"It's perfectly true," he said, "that my word is not law around here as it once was." Mr. Brady felt that this was due in part to the fact that the children were getting older, but he feels also that his unemployment must have a lot to do with it, in addition. "When they see me hanging around the house all the time and know that I can't find work, it has its effect all right. I guess the children never expect to see me work again."

His unemployment has made the children feel independent. His working son, 17, seemed to have become old overnight. "The son of twenty-two is just like a father around the house. He tries to settle any little brother-and-sister fights and even encourages me and my wife."

Mr. Brady spoke of changes in the attitude of the children

without bitterness, assuring the interviewer that they were good children, and that it was only natural for children to lose respect for an unemployed father. It appears that Mr. Brady finds his religion and prestige in the mission a balm for the loss of status with the children.

Mrs. Brady said that the burden of bringing up the children has always been hers. Mr. Brady had a very vicious temper and "whipped terribly hard." Since being "saved," Mr. Brady has become gentler and sweeter. Now the threat of whipping usually suffices because the children know he whips very hard, but he doesn't bother much with disciplining.

Mrs. Brady was somewhat evasive in her interview and did not admit any loss of respect on the part of the children. "Of course," she said, "the 17-year-old son is working and must be given more consideration. Everyone gets discouraged and irritable and sometimes the children get snappy. If we egged them on, there would be no end of arguments. We just keep quiet."

The best information on changes came from the children themselves. John, 22, impressed the interviewer as an easygoing, pleasant but lazy young man. He has looked for work but has not been able to find anything worth taking. He might find a job for $7.00, but "Hell, working all week for $7.00! There's no percentage in that."

John says that his father certainly lost control of the children. When his father was working—"when he was in the dough, his word was law. If you didn't like it, you got a sock in the jaw." If he had talked to his father four years ago the way Henry, the 17-year-old brother, talks to him now, his father would have "killed him."

When John was sixteen, he was helping his father repair a car. "Oh, you don't know any more about this than I do," he said. His father flung a hammer at him which laid him out. His father wouldn't dare to pull that now with his working brother. What's more, he wouldn't want to. "He is too discouraged and doesn't give a damn like he used to."

John told another incident. The father and two sons were working on the car. The father asked Henry to get a tool from the kitchen. "What do you think I am, your flunky?" answered Henry. He was not punished. At another time Henry was going out to see his girl. His father said, "Why don't you stay at home—it costs too much to go out so often." Henry said, "It's none of your business how much money I spend.

It's mine. You keep your nose out of it." And his father was silent.

Only once in a great while does his father's old temper return. A couple of months ago Henry came from work in a bad humor and started cussing at the dinner table. His father told him to shut up. Henry mumbled something to the effect that his father should "go to the Devil." His father jumped out of his chair and went for Henry with his fists. But such things happen very seldom. In a couple of hours he was good-natured again.

Sometimes when the father says "Good morning," Henry might answer "Go on—don't bother me." Henry has more to say than anyone else as to the expenditure of money. John says the change is very noticeable, because before the depression his father was the big boss. Now, if they get to arguing about money, Henry tells his father to bring in some money if he wants to kick so much.

Again, at times they have arguments over the food. Their mother might buy something for supper which their father didn't like; frankfurters, for example. His father would kick about it and feel that he was being discriminated against. "But money is the boss around here." Henry does more for the family than anyone else, so they cannot go against his wishes too much.

John summarized his attitude by saying, "I don't know that I have lost respect for the old man the way Henry has. I guess I sort of pity him. I feel like I want to help him. I'll tell you how it is. I feel he is more my equal than he used to be."

Henry is tall and thin. He appeared sulky and ill-humored to the interviewer. "The old man was right handy with his fists," he said, in describing his childhood. "I guess I got more than my share of what was coming to me. He used to get mad at me all the time. Whenever he said something, he wanted it done right away. If you didn't do it, he'd go for you. He was a pretty good father, I guess. He was very liberal with the kids and cheerful. He'd give you the shirt off his back, but we sure got plenty of lickings. He has calmed down a lot since he started going to the Pentecost mission. Besides, I'm my own boss now. Nobody can tell me what to do or how to spend my money. Working makes you feel independent. I remind them who makes the money. They don't say much. They just take it, that's all. *I'm* not the one on relief. I can't help feeling that way."

Henry said that seeing his father so discouraged and without ambition made him lose respect for him. "He is not the same father, that's all. You can't help not looking up to him like we used to. None of us is afraid of him like we used to be. That's natural, isn't it?"

The interviewer witnessed the following incident:

A peddler came and asked Mr. Brady for 8 cents for a head of cabbage that Mrs. Brady had bought. Henry tossed the peddler a dime. The peddler handed him 2 cents change, but Henry, indicating his father with a toss of his head, said, "Give them to him." Mr. Brady took the 2 cents silently.

Another incident occurred when the family was sitting around the dinner table. The family was almost finished with dinner when Henry came in. Mr. Brady got up immediately and surrendered his place at the table to him. There was no extra chair. Henry took the place at the table as a matter of fact without thanking his father for it.

The reaction of the two sons differed, but in both cases we witness change in attitudes towards the father as loss of respect and loss of fear. Furthermore, we observe complete loss of control over the children. Not only is the father helpless with regard to his sons' activities (his sons' going out too often and staying out too late, etc.), but he must meekly accept indignities, particularly from his working son.

The Robinson and Dorrance families tell very much the same story.

It is interesting to note that in families in which the role of the provider is taken over by one of the children the parents themselves often attempt to protect the authority of the working child. The parents are apparently afraid that if the wage-earning son is not treated well he might leave the family, thus withdrawing his support.

The Robinson boy, 17 years old, testified as follows:

"One thing," said he quite spontaneously, "we three younger kids were told to be nice to John and Edward. We were not supposed to argue with them at all because they were bringing in the dough."

The Brady family just described illustrates the same situation. The interview with the mother, the father, and the son revealed the indulgence of the parents towards the working son. The daughter said in her interview, "Henry thinks he is the king all right, supporting the family and all that, and the folks humor him along."

In conclusion we shall summarize the aspects of unemployment which proved critical in the disruption of the father's and the husband's authority. Tables 12 and 13 present the results.

TABLE 12

FEATURES OF UNEMPLOYMENT LEADING TO THE MAN'S LOSS OF STATUS WITH CHILDREN, ADOLESCENTS, AND WIVES

	Number of Individuals		
	Children 12 to 15	Adolescents 15 and Over	Wives
Failure of man as a provider and loss of money	1	9	10
Changes in the man and presence at home	5	4	3
Unknown	1	4	0
Totals	7	17	13

TABLE 13

	Children 15 Years Old and Over	
	Employed	Not Employed
Failure of man as a provider and loss of money	6	3
Changes in the man and presence at home	1	3
Unknown	—	4
Totals	7	10

The sharpest difference in the process of deterioration of authority appears between the younger children and the wife. It was the loss of prestige and the loss of economic power implied in unemployment which disrupted the husband's status. Not so with the children. The lowered social prestige of the unemployed man had apparently no influence upon the attitude of the child. For only one child among all children under 15 was the father's loss of a job in itself a cause of the change in attitudes. The loss of authority with the younger child was due to changes in personal relations with the father, brought about by certain indirect effects of unemployment, particularly changes in the father's behavior towards the child.

For the unemployed adolescent the direct role of unemployment is as unimportant as for the younger child. It is only when unemployment leads to certain indirect effects that it becomes dangerous to the father's authority.

For the gainfully employed children the critical factors in the loss of the father's authority lay in his loss of money and in the interchange of economic roles. It is understandable why the presence of the father at home and changes in his personality should have proved of less importance to a working child who himself is away from home and independent of the father's control.

With regard to the process of loss there are many illustrations of the same cumulative character of conflicts as was observed in marital relations. In the Brady family, for example, the girl of sixteen keenly felt economic privations and talked frequently about them. Her complaints disturbed her father. He saw in them an accusation and a threat to his status. "The kids are getting too fresh" he said to his wife who hitherto had complete charge of the children: "I think I'd better take things into my own hands." His first acts as a disciplinarian were to impose all kinds of restrictions: he was to pass upon all the friends before his daughter could go out with them, she wasn't to stay out after 11 o'clock; whenever she uttered any complaint she had to stay in. Needless to say, his steps to arrest the loss of his authority served only to further it. Now the girl really became resentful towards the father. Her resentment and impertinence irritated him still further.

A similar process is observed in another family. In contrast to the first case, however, there is no evidence whatsoever that the father's increased irritability was in itself a reaction to the threat of loss of authority. It was most probably a reaction to other features of unemployment. He was a pedantic and sadistic man with many stubborn notions about how the household affairs should be conducted. Being at home all day, he exerted continuous pressure upon the girl, nagging her from morning to night. This antagonized her. She reacted to her father's increased irritability with impertinence and disobedience. Her reaction, in turn, was a source of further irritation to her father. In both families the deterioration of the father's status took the form of a circular process in which the reactions of the child served only to arouse the father to still further attacks.

Unemployment has undermined the father's authority in some families but not in others. In this section we shall deal with some factors that determine the differences in the vulnerability of the father's authority to unemployment.

WHAT DETERMINES THE STANDING OF THE UNEMPLOYED FATHER WITH HIS ADOLESCENT CHILD

In order to understand the reactions of the adolescent to the unemployed father we must first consider the extent to which he experiences hardships as the result of unemployment. Unemployment may not affect the child's attitude in some cases because it does not bring about any special hardship. In other cases the child may experience difficulties but for various reasons maintain his attitude towards the father.

Among the conditions which may be expected to determine how much of a hardship unemployment imposes upon a child are the *personality and interests of the child.*

Children vary with regard to their interests. Some adolescents have desires and ambitions which are especially likely to be frustrated by the unemployment of the father. Others are less affected by the poverty of the family. An attractive 16-year-old girl in the Burke family was mature for her age. All the other members of the family called her "boy-crazy." The one dominant interest of her life was to be well dressed and popular with the boys. She was forever demanding new clothes, and the poverty of the family defeated her in her main ambition in life.

On the other hand, the 19-year-old girl in another family was extremely attached to her mother. In fact, her parents had to urge her to go out and mingle with young people instead of staying at home with her mother all the time. The problem of inadequate clothes was not uppermost in her mind.

In two cases, the children were much devoted to hobbies which were acceptable to the parents and were not expensive. These children did not feel the depression very keenly.

In the attempt to classify the children with regard to their interests we have been able to distinguish only the extreme cases: Those with interests much frustrated by the depression like the girl in the Burke family, and those with interests very little affected by the depression like the 19-year-old girl described above. The largest group of children was found between the two extremes. No precise tests of interests were used to enable us to make finer distinctions. Table 14 sums up the relation of interests to the effects of unemployment upon the father's authority.

TABLE 14

Frustrated Interests	Loss	No Loss
Few......................	0	8
Average..................	10	33
Many.....................	7	2
Totals...............	17	43

It appears from the table that the more a particular adolescent suffers from the depression, the greater the likelihood of deterioration of relations with the father.

The temperament of the child may be another conditioning factor. A phlegmatic and docile child may react differently to the greater irritability of the father than a nervous and sensitive child. Unfortunately no personality tests were employed to enable us to check this hypothesis.

So far we have dealt with the extent to which the depression is experienced as a hardship by a particular adolescent. There is some indication that the more the child suffers from the depression the greater the likelihood of deterioration of parental relations. But this does not tell the whole story. Unemployment might bring much suffering to the adolescent without affecting his relation with his father. On the other hand we have cases in which the depression does not apparently present a great shock to the adolescent and yet the relations with the father have deteriorated. We must look for other factors in the problem. One such factor is the character of predepression father-child relations.

Kinds of Father-Child Relations.[17] A comparison of the loss

[17] To ascertain the vulnerability of various kinds of father-child relations to unemployment it would have been desirable to duplicate the procedure followed in marital relations and to test the relative frequency of various kinds of relations among the loss and the no-loss cases. It proved difficult, however, to do so. The reason lies partly in the questionnaire. The interviewers were not instructed to consider the predepression parental relations in the same detail as the predepression marital relations. Un-

and no loss cases suggests that certain kinds of father-child relations withstood unemployment better than others.

Among the fathers whose status was not affected by unemployment there were some who, prior to unemployment, were strong and others who were weak, some who were strict and authoritarian and others who were liberal and noninterfering, some who had the superior authority of the two parents and others who were dominated by the mothers. But in all cases they had one thing in common—the personal relations between father and child were satisfactory. The child had confidence in the father, and there was some companionship between the two. Even when there was no admiration for the father, there was affection for him and absence of resentment. The absence of resentment against the father, whatever that in itself may be due to, is a salient feature in most of the no-loss cases.[18]

There was one group of families in which the father had succeeded in keeping his status, even though he did not build up particularly satisfactory relations with his children. Those were the cases in which strong family folkways demanded certain deference to the father. The general attitude of these families is "The father is a father and must be obeyed. No well-brought-up children would think of behaving disrespect-

---

doubtedly it would have been possible to devise questions revealing the educational policy and practices as well as other aspects of parental relations in greater detail. However, even an improved questionnaire may not have yielded adequate information for the younger children. The child's attitudes are not sufficiently crystallized and verbalized to enable him to reconstruct preunemployment relations. Furthermore, it may be quite undesirable to press the child too much into verbalizing certain attitudes.

The difficulty of ascertaining preunemployment parent-child relations refers largely to the loss cases. If the interview did not reveal any changes in parental relations, then we assume that the preunemployment relations were the same as those at the time of the interview.

In view of these difficulties, we have not attempted any systematic count of the relative frequency of the various kinds of parent-child relations in the loss and no-loss cases. Neither can we claim that we have discerned the conditions accounting for loss or preservation of authority. It is only with regard to the decisive features that discerning has been carried through with thoroughness. The discussion is based upon the hypotheses derived from the analysis of individual cases or comparisons of pairs of loss and no-loss cases.

[18] It is interesting that in a number of cases the fathers were very strict and authoritarian without, however, engendering any resentment in the child. Apparently the child can stand a good deal of interference with his wishes provided it is done in a certain way.

fully to a father merely because he lost his job." To be more specific, there are three kinds of father-child relations which are frequently found among the no-loss cases. Indeed, of the 46 adolescents who exhibit no change in attitude toward the father, over three-fifths belong to these three types. While, as was already indicated, it was not always possible to reconstruct the past in the loss cases, it appears that these types were much less frequent in the loss cases. These three types are: *an authoritative and interested father who is admired by the child, a kindly and noninterfering father for whom the child has affection,* and *a patriarchal family organization accepted by the child.*

When we turn now to fathers whose authority deteriorated because of their unemployment, we again find that father-child relations fall into certain groups. Frequent among the loss cases is the father who was coercive and completely disinterested in the children. He may have had authority prior to unemployment, but it was based to a great extent upon fear. He was a *coercive and disinterested father feared by the child.*

Among the loss cases there was still another kind of father-child relations. In some families there was a complete lack of understanding between parents and children. It was due to the fact that parents who were "old-fashioned" attempted to impose regulations which were completely out of harmony with the children's environment. They were unintelligent parents and did not command the respect of their children in their own right. The children regarded their parents chiefly as a hindrance. This type may be described as *utilitarian obedience to an unintelligent and interfering father.*

Such were the dominant kinds of relations distinguished among the loss and no-loss cases. We shall describe these types in greater detail and indicate how they combine with certain other factors to make the unemployed father's status secure or insecure. We shall consider first the types which are found more frequently among the no-loss cases and which appear to be least susceptible to unemployment.

An Authoritative and Interested Father Admired by the Child. Most parents have some attachment and devotion to their children, but not many apparently enjoy the children's world for its own sake. The fathers belonging to this group show a profound interest in the child's personality, his play, his ambitions. The companionship that exists between the father and the children is manifested in such incidents as the following: The father plays games with the children, talks to them at great length about their own interests and problems, serves as an arbiter in their quarrels or contests. The children in one family begged their father to arrange his WPA work so that his leisure hours would coincide with theirs.

These fathers are not merely interested in their children but show insight into and understanding of the children's personalities. "My son," said one father, "is a rough-and-ready type who doesn't think anything of an argument or a fight. It's no use hitting this kind. You have to reason with him." His wife does not understand the boy, but he does. Another father described the difference between his two children as follows:

"Betty (aged 7) is a dependable girl, a regular little lady. She likes to be independent, and she doesn't want you to explain too much. When I send her to do some errands, I don't explain too much because I know that she prefers it that way. Carl (aged 6) is different. You have to explain everything to him and then he often disobeys my orders. But I figured out that he disobeys not out of mischief, but because he is daydreaming. I can just see that he gets interested in something and forgets what I have told him."

Firmness and consistency characterize the educational policy of these fathers. They are firm fathers and expect obedience. It is no use trying to wheedle things out of them. When they give an order they never weaken. One father says that he makes it a sacred rule never to promise anything that he cannot fulfill. He never puts the children off with a promise just to get rid of them. The firmness, however, is not stubbornness or inflexibility, because the fathers exhibit considerable tact in disciplining. They seem to know how far they can assert their will without engendering seeds of humiliation and rebellion. One 16-year-old girl was guilty of some rather severe misbehavior. The most obvious punishment in that particular case would have been to deny her a school picnic to which she had been looking forward with great eagerness. The father said to the interviewer that, although the girl deserved this punishment, he substituted another because he felt that it would make her too bitter.

Another characteristic of these fathers is their self-control. One wife said that when her husband got irritated he put on his hat and walked around the block because he did not want his children to suffer from his irritability. Another woman said that her husband controlled his temper with the children because he was afraid that they would lose respect for him if he became cranky. One father tells the following story. He once saw his little girl playing with a playmate of whom he disapproved. Instead of making a scene then and there or taking her home, he waited until she returned and then discussed the whole matter with her. Still another father of this group says that, while he spanks the children, he tries not to hit them when he is tired or irritated. It is always for some specific misbehavior.

About one-sixth of the adolescents who did not change their attitude toward the father belonged to the kind of families described above. It appears that through firmness, tact, and companionship with the children, these fathers have succeeded in building up secure personal relations. Loss of the father's status in the outside world, loss of money as means of control, was not fraught with danger for the father because of his success in personal contacts with his children.

We do not mean to imply that such relations are under no circumstances affected by unemployment. Among the loss cases there is one, for example, that seems to have been characterized by the relations just described, and yet the attitude toward the father has changed. In this case, however, the father has become nervous, irritable, and, indeed, cruel to the family. The daughter says that she can hardly believe that her father is the same person that he used to be. It may also be that a radical change in marital relations may endanger the father's status even where it was securely based upon personal friendship as in this kind of relation.

The second kind of father-child relation that occurs frequently among the no-loss cases is quite different from the type just described. It is the affection for a kindly, rather weak, and noninterfering father.

A kindly and noninterfering father for whom the child has affection: In cases which fall under this type the father did not have high authority prior to unemployment, and the dominant attitude of the children toward the father is not admiration, but affection. The families are matriarchal families, and the mother provides the traditionally masculine authoritarian policy. The following features characterize the behavior and attitude of these fathers towards their children:

The fathers are lenient and do not attempt much interference in the children's lives.

The fathers are interested in their children and are fond of them.

Even when the fathers have certain wishes concerning the children, they do not assert much pressure to realize them. Thus, one father would like his daughter to complete high school, but he says, "After all, what's the use of insisting if the child isn't interested?" In another family, the father and the mother have a few minor disagreements as to the educational policy, but he says, "What's the use of kicking up an argument over it?" This lack of assertiveness in the fathers is not accompanied by resentment on their part. They give in simply because they don't think the issues at stake are very critical. While the fathers do not attempt to exercise much regulation over their children's lives, they are interested in the children and are fond of them. One wife says that her husband is "bighearted with the children and is always joking with them." He is a step-father, but she says that a real father couldn't be better to them than he is. In yet another family the father lies down with the children because they don't like to go to sleep alone.

It is reasonable that this kind of parental relations will also be unaffected by unemployment. First of all, one might point out that the change which could occur in such families would lie not so much in the emancipation from the father's control as in change in attitudes. The fathers exercise so little regulation of the children that the changes in control would be imperceptible. The change could occur in growth of contempt for the father manifested in impertinence towards him, frequent reminders of his unemployment, complete disregard of his wishes, and alienation from him.

We do not observe any such changes. Invariably, the children absolve the fathers from blame for unemployment and show more or less sympathy for his plight.

There is perhaps no reason for disintegration of relations in such cases. The fathers were never a hindrance to the children in the pursuit of their desires. These children did not have to submit to the fathers against their wills. There is no motive, then, for them to utilize their fathers' weakness in order to assert their own power.

There is nothing in the situation to prevent the children from feeling some loss of respect for the fathers because of their unemployment. As a matter of fact, this actually may have been the case. But because there is no hostility towards the fathers, the children are not likely to give it overt manifestations. That is why it is not easy to detect even if it does exist.

In conclusion, it might be interesting to inquire whether such kinds of father-child relations are completely secure and under no conditions show change. If the father thinks that it is natural for an unemployed father to lose the respect of the children, and this attitude undermines his self-respect, it, in turn, may lower his status. In one family the father was kindly, well liked, and noninterfering. His wife describes changes in him by saying that he was always meek, but since unemployment he had become meeker than ever, and anyone could "walk over him." There is some evidence that this changed attitude of the man affected the parental relations.

Another seed of destruction in a family of this kind is a change in the attitude of the mother. In one case, the woman had complete control of the children. Since the depression she shows resentment against her husband, and her loss of respect for him apparently affected the father's status with the children.

The Patriarchal Pattern and Parental Relations. The third kind of family among the no-loss cases was one characterized by the patriarchal attitudes towards the father. In about one-fourth of all the no-loss adolescents that was the case. In such cases there was no evidence of admiration or affection for the father, no special companionship with him. What appeared as a deterrent in those families was the general atmosphere in the family: "The father is a father and he must be obeyed. No well-brought-up children would think of behaving disrepectfully towards a father merely because he has lost his job."

The father in one family is not a particularly intelligent disciplinarian. He imposes what seem unduly "old-fashioned" and oppressive regulations upon his 16-year-old girl. The girl, however, is not at all rebellious. There is some conflict with her father over the curfew, but on the whole she accepts his right to assert authority. To the question, "Does your father help with the housework?" she said, "Why should he? It isn't a man's job."

In another case, the father, though concerned about his children, is quite remote from their world and is certainly not a companion to them. His working son, 23 years old, does not smoke in his father's presence and goes into the bathroom if he wants a cigarette.

The father in still another family is very hot-tempered and has become more irritable since unemployment. His 15-year-old girl is forbidden to go out with boys. There is conflict over it, but again acceptance of the father's position—indeed, a good deal of consideration for him. The children, after several years of their father's unemployment, would not sit down to dinner without him.

In one case, the father is not interested in the children and is rather uncouth in comparison with the rest of the family. And yet there is no blame for his unemployment, and he is treated as the head of the family.

It is interesting to note that in all cases in which patriarchal traditions safeguarded the father's status, the mother's attitude towards the father has not deteriorated since unemployment. Perhaps it is only with the support of the mother that the man can keep his status with the children.

Such were the types found frequently among the no-loss cases. Other kinds of relations on the other hand were more frequent among the loss cases. One such relation was fear of a coercive father.

Coercive and Unconcerned Father, Feared by the Child. The cases included in this group were characterized by highly unsatisfactory father-child relations. These fathers were not interested in their children. Indeed, in some cases the father, in the words of both his wife and the children, "acted as if he hated his children." While there was practically no friendly contact between the father and the children, now and then there were outbursts of irritation on the part of the father. The children were afraid to disobey him. Thus, of the father in one family of two boys, the wife says that he is cruel to the children, particularly to the older boy. The mother cannot protect the children from the father's violence as much as she would like to because she, herself, is afraid of him. He beats her. Since unemployment the father has been more irritable with the children. After an unsuccessful day of job-hunting, the children know that they have to keep out of his way. The father confesses that he regrets ever getting married and having children. He says that if he had it to do over again he would not marry so young a woman.

The father in another case is not interested in his children. His attractive girls, twins, complain that he never says "Hello" to them when he meets them on the street, and they are humiliated to have their friends witness their father's indifference towards them. His only contact with his girls consists in strict and unreasonable regulations of their recreation. He beats them if they disobey him. They do, however, disobey him behind his back, with their mother's knowledge.

This coercive and unconcerned father tended to lose his control over the children for one or more of the following reasons:

a. This kind of man is likely to become still more irritable and coercive as the result of unemployment.
b. Children invariably blame him for unemployment because they have sufficient resentment against him to seize this opportunity to condemn him.
c. If they are older and ready to work, they take advantage of their economic independence and the dependence of the father to settle past grievances.
d. If unemployment affects the father so as to break down his self-esteem, and thus his force in demanding obedience, he is likely to lose all authority, because it is only force which maintained it in the first place.

There are circumstances under which this coercive and unconcerned father succeeded in keeping his preunemployment status. In one case, it was the timidity and introversion of the child that explained the absence of overt changes in relations. The boy is 13 years old, a shy, rather dull, timid child. Since the depression he has withdrawn from his playmates. He says that his father has become more nervous, but he keeps from getting hit too often by getting out of his father's way. Preunemployment relations presented much the same picture.

In another family certain improvements in the father explained the preservation of his status. He used to drink prior to the depression, and the whole family was in fear of him. His daughter, 17 years old, said, "Father used to drink and holler a lot. Now he is quieter. However, he is still the boss in the family. He would break our necks if he heard us saying anything disrespectful about him." The children mind their father in the few strict regulations that he imposes.

There is another pattern of parental relations which is frequent among the loss cases. It may be described perhaps as *utilitarian obedience to an interfering father*. In these families there was a gulf between the parents and children. The children considered the parents old-fashioned and had no respect for them. There were always quarrels because the parents attempted to impose regulations that were out of harmony with the children's folkways. In some cases the conflicts resulted not from outmoded regulations of the parents, but from the selfish and unreasonable demands of the children. Whatever caused it, the fathers in these families were regarded chiefly as a hindrance to the children in the pursuit of their own interests. The authority that the fathers had prior to unemployment depended partly on the youth of the children and their economic dependence. When unemployment came, all parents in this group complained that with loss of money they lost all means of controlling their children. In such families, when the children started to earn, they went their own way with complete indifference to their parents' desires.

Mother's Attitude towards the Father as a Factor in Parental Relations. In the discussion of father-child relations, reference has already been made to the importance of the mother's attitude towards the father. To keep his authority with the children the man has to maintain it with his wife. Apparently the father does not rule alone. His prestige needs the mother's endorsement. Table 15 summarizes the relation between loss in marital and parental relations.

TABLE 15

LOSS OF AUTHORITY IN MARITAL AND PARENTAL RELATIONS

Wife	Children Loss *	Children No Loss	Total
Loss...........	9	4	13
No loss.........	8	37	45
Unknown.......	—	—	1
Totals.......	17	41	59

* Number of families in which one or more children changed their attitude towards the father.

Out of 13 loss cases in marital relations, 9 are also loss cases in parental relations. Out of 45 no-loss cases in marital relations, only 8 are loss cases in parental relations. The mere fact that the change in the man's status tends to occur in both spheres does not, of course, in itself prove that the critical factor is the attitude of the wife. But when the deterioration in the man's status was restricted to one sphere, it was more likely to be the parental sphere. Loss in marital relations alone was less frequent.

It can be readily understood why the man's status with his children would depend upon his standing with his wife. The father's authority is in many cases derived from the prestige with which the family endows the role of the father. The mother's contempt for the father is likely to weaken the child's acceptance of the traditional pattern. The husband's authority, on the other hand, does not depend so much upon his success with the children. It depends to a lesser extent upon traditional factors than on personality configurations, and these are less likely to be affected by the children's revolt. Besides, the mother feels herself an ally of the father in his attempt to maintain discipline. Their revolt threatens her status as well.

These considerations are confirmed by a detailed examination of the four cases in which growing contempt for the husband on the part of the wife did not drag parental authority with it into the abyss. In one of those cases, there was marital strife and a clear-cut alignment of the older children against the mother. Under such circumstances, criticism of the father would naturally tend to make the children rally to their father's support. In other cases, the attitude towards the father was that of affection. The relations were of the kind described as affection for a kindly noninterfering father. It may have been that the mother's increased contempt diminished in subtle ways what little admiration the children did have, but the present attitude of the children is that of sympathy for the father and devotion to him.

In still another case, no change was recorded in parental relations for a particular reason. In the Adams family, the mother had always been dominant in the control of the children. The children had almost no contact with the father, who was a drunkard. The mother's liberation from the father's coercion had no immediate effect upon the children.

7

OTHER EFFECTS OF UNEMPLOYMENT

UPON FAMILY LIFE

THE POLITICAL ATTITUDES OF UNEMPLOYED WORKERS

WHAT does the unemployed man think of the socio-economic system? Has unemployment changed his political outlook? Has it aroused doubts in him as to the capitalistic system and his place within it? Is he embittered against the system?

Depression and unemployment rudely shattered his feeling of economic and social security. Again and again the man said, "If someone had told me five or six years ago that I would be accepting relief, I would have knocked his teeth out." "I didn't think that things like this (relief) would be necessary for people of our kind." "I never thought it could happen to us."

But although discouraged and despondent over their economic difficulties, these men did not become the class-conscious radicals some expected them to become. This is, of course, due to their background, their economic and social position before the depression, and the views they held at that time.

We must remind the reader that the men in our group did not belong to the industrial proletariat. They formed what might, in a way, be termed a marginal group between the proletariat and the lower middle class. Both from the point of view of their economic status and their ideology, they were nearer to the middle class than they were to the worker. Many of the men were artisans who worked for contractors, carpenters, automobile mechanics, painters, plumbers. A few worked for large con-

116

cerns. This type of economic activity would tend to develop in them the general individualistic traditions typical of the American middle class. The industrial worker, working in a large concern, performing a specified task in a vast and complicated series of operations, is more likely to develop a feeling of individual impotence. The relation between his particular operation and the finished product is mediated by many processes and operations of which he has often only a vague notion. He cannot feel any control over the whole enterprise in which he is engaged. On the contrary, this enterprise appears to him vast, mysterious, and overpowering. The men in our study, on the other hand, worked alone or in small groups. Their relation to the job was such as to increase their self-confidence and feeling of importance: they possessed a craft that required training; they did a job from the beginning to the end, seeing clearly the relation between their work and the completed product. Their relation to the whole enterprise was such as to give them a greater sense of control.

There was a further characteristic of the economic position of these men, and that was the possibility of economic progress. The gulf between their own position and that of the contractor was not so great. Many of them had hopes of being able to establish themselves in business and become bosses instead of employees.

The immediate relation of these craftsmen to the product of their labor, the relative simplicity of the whole economic enterprise, the very simple division of labor, the possibility of becoming an independent entrepreneur—all of these circumstances have furthered a typically middle-class outlook. Most of the men, prior to unemployment, apparently accepted the socioeconomic system. On the whole, they were little concerned with politics. A few were members of the Democratic or the Republican political club. Their lives centered around the hopes of raising the standard of living of the family, of acquiring a car, or perhaps a home, bringing up the children in some comfort, or perhaps putting them through high school. These factors explain why, although the experiences of the depression shocked these men so that they lost some of their hope, the majority of them did not change their fundamental class notions. Notwithstanding the experiences of the depression, a small group of men still thought they were at fault. The system had nothing to do with it. They would have succeeded had they been more capable or tried harder. A few men, however, did not place the blame on themselves, but found a scapegoat for their troubles. The system was all right, but some force or person in it spoiled its perfect working. Others were simply resigned. Still others desired a reform within capitalism. In only one-sixth of the cases was there an inkling of attitudes changing towards the left. We shall illustrate the various attitudes mentioned above.

It is up to the man. The individualistic attitudes of this group of men were so remarkably strong that after four years of insistent but futile search for work some men in the group put the responsibility for unemployment on their own shoulders. One marvels at the strength of the traditional social attitude that would make some of these men, who looked for work tirelessly, week in and week out, for three or four years, still cling to the belief that it is "up to the man."

"I would like you to put it down in black and white," said Mr. Adams, "that I am to blame for my present state. It isn't the system. The system is all right. It's me. I had plenty of opportunities to have a decent life among my own class of people. It was drink that ruined me." He thinks that the "man in the White House" is ruining the country. He is getting the country in debt. Though this man is unemployed, he does not believe in relief, for he is sure he could get along without it, and believes that it just pauperizes the people. He continued, "A young man can get a job if he wants to work. Take my son— he could hang around the corner, but instead he goes up to the golf course and to the bowling alley and makes a dollar. Anyone with stamina can make something of himself even now."

Another man said, "Depression is just a handy phrase in the mouths of a lot of people who like to lay back and make the world give them a living." This man blames himself for not having prepared himself better for life when he was young and had opportunities. After the depression he fell sick, and it is his ill health, he feels, that accounts in part for his unemployment. If he had had more education, he would have been fitted for indoor work and thus not handicapped so much by poor health.

This view was held also by another man, who said that he would not have been unemployed if he had taken advantage of his early opportunities. He could have gone to school and got his education, and educated people have not suffered from the depression as much as others have. It is his own lack of ambition that got him down.

Another self-blaming man feels that he had had some pretty

good breaks during his life time, but didn't make the most of them. He inherited some money, but was careless and invested it in a trucking business with a crook who cheated him out of all his fortune.

THE SCAPEGOAT FOR UNEMPLOYMENT

Another quite different reaction is to find a scapegoat. In contrast to the attitude just described, many men experienced a deep sense of injustice regarding their unemployment. They also show a violent hatred. This hatred is directed to particular groups which appeared to the men to have caused the trouble.

Insurance companies and the employment of married women were blamed by a former detective. He said, "I should like to get all the directors of insurance companies and shoot them with my own hands. It's their fault that a man over forty can't be employed. What is a man supposed to do? Go to the kitchen and turn on the gas? Insurance directors keep on getting $50,-000 a year when they are fifty or sixty years old." He claimed also that another cause of the depression was married women working. There should be a law prohibiting the wife from taking a position if her husband is employed. Millions of jobs would be open to men who have families to support if such a law went into effect.

Other men find causes of the depression and therefore the objects of their hatred in other groups and conditions as, for example, the foreigners. If the foreigners were sent back, there would be more jobs left for Americans. "Just look at the street cars in the morning," said one of them, "they are filled with Italians and colored people. The Italians, Irish, and colored people somehow get the preference."

The scapegoats are in some cases even more remotely connected with the causes of the depression. Some of the unemployed have concentrated all their hatred upon the relief investigators or the head of the relief office. Why should these girls keep their jobs? Why shouldn't the relief investigators be recruited from the unemployed? Some of the investigators are rich girls who live at home and have cars of their own. Why should heads of relief offices get so much money? These statements were supplemented by long lists of grievances against the relief investigators.

Another difficulty was felt by Mr. Jones. "There would be no unemployment in N——— if a law was passed forbidding

outsiders to get N——— jobs. My blood boils when I pass by
the railroad depot in the morning and see all of those people
from the outside coming to N——— to work."

And one of the men wants a revolution to get the crooked
politicians out of the government and put honest people in
instead.

Resignation. Still another reaction is that of resignation.
Several men commented:

"The world is in a mess, but there is nothing that I, or anybody
else, can do about it. Human nature is human nature. Put the
socialists in the government and there will be just as much graft
and corruption."

"No other system will work any better."

"What can be done about it? Just make the best of it and
wait—perhaps the cycle will change and times will be better."

"We've always had cycles of depression and prosperity, and
we'll continue to have them."

"Socialism will be no solution. You divide the money up
equally, and in a little while some will have more than the
others and we'll be just where we are now."

Somewhat related to this attitude of resignation is a feeling
expressed by two of the men that "it's all luck and fate. Some
men have all the luck in the world and others don't." They
feel they had luck themselves, but that it turned. They feel a
stretch of good luck is due them again.

Reforms within Capitalism. A group of men felt that the
depression showed certain defects in capitalism which might be
remedied by some particular measure, leaving the system intact,
however. Schemes like unemployment insurance, higher wages
which would tide the laboring man through the depression, the
New Deal, the return to Republican policies that would start the
industry going and put the country back on its feet, were some
of the changes suggested by the men within the program of the
Republican or the Democratic party.

Toward the left. Out of the group of 59 men, 10 testified to a
change in their point of view towards the left. We included
among the 10 two or three who, without using the word "socialism," expressed some resentment in class terms. One man who
was articulate and bitter expressed his attitudes in words very
much like the following:

"At first we believed in Roosevelt. When we heard him the
day after election over the radio talking about the 'forgotten
man,' we thought, 'here's a man who will save us.' It was after

election, so we figured he didn't have to say it if he didn't
mean it. But it certainly turned out to be 'a raw deal.' Someone said on the radio the other day, 'let the neighbors help.'
Well, my neighbors are as poor as I am. The neighbors who
could help me don't live near me.

"There's a small clique in this country that's well off, and
we're on the outside. It's a rotten hook-up. It can't be much
worse. If it's Communism that will give us jobs, I say 'let us
have Communism.' My solution? Take the money away from
the rich—they can't eat it for breakfast, can they? They put
it in the bank instead of starting things going. There's many a
man going by in a car that needs fixing. If he could afford it,
he'd have it fixed. Then I'd have the money to pay a doctor
so my boy wouldn't have to cough for a whole week without
anybody examining him, and I would start papering this house
and fixing it and giving the work to others.

"Sometimes I think I may join some party (radical). At
least it may make a dent in the right direction. Maybe it will
make things easier for the kids."

Indignant as the men were against the "rich" and against
"capitalism," they clung to the old concept of their social role
and only reluctantly identified themselves with the rebels.
Prior to unemployment they had belonged, or had had the illu-
sion of belonging, to the "insiders." They were not as rich as
some others, but neither were they the malcontents and the
"have nots." The country was theirs, the government was theirs,
the policeman was their agent in dealing with troublemakers.

Mrs. Baldwin expressed these attitudes vividly when she said,

"Why should there be so many rich people when we don't even
have enough food sometimes. I feel so mad about it that I
could go out and shoot people, but *I hate to think of myself as
a radical.* When I was young, I thought that anarchists were
just the most awful people, but now I think that they are on the
right track because nobody else cares for the suppressed people."

Her husband added that he heard someone saying over the
radio what a wonderful thing this relief is. "Why, the colored
people down south have more food than they ever had." He
went on to say, "That certainly made me boil. Where do I
come in to be compared with those colored people? They have
always lived like animals. It may be good for them, but they
can't class me with the colored."

While the men in this group expressed some resentment
against "capitalism," they were not prepared to take radical

action. After the vehement denunciation of capitalism by the
unemployed man cited above, we asked whom he would vote
for at the next election. He answered, "It may seem funny to
you after what I have said, but I'll vote Republican. You see,
the Republicans are the moneyed people. They have got all
the money, but now they hide it away. I think that if we put
them back they will start the factories going. We will at least
have a steady job."

THE SOCIAL LIFE OF THE UNEMPLOYED

The unemployed man and his wife have no social life outside
the family. The extent of the social isolation of the family is
truly striking. This refers not only to formal club affiliations
but also to informal social life. The typical family in our group
does not attend church, does not belong to clubs, and for
months at a time does not have social contacts with anyone
outside the family. Furthermore, the families do not give
the impression of maintaining any ties with the community as
a whole.

Family after family gave the same story of meager social
contacts.

In the Gessell family, the husband and the wife are 55 and 53
years old respectively. Three of their five children live at home.
Neither Mr. nor Mrs. Gessell attends church. Mr. Gessell be-
longs to the plumbers' union, but is not active in it and never
attends meetings. He does not belong to any clubs. Neither
does Mrs. Gessell. It has been years, says Mrs. Gessell, since
they have been out together. The last occasion was the funeral
of a very old friend. They have no friends in the neighborhood.
The neighborhood has deteriorated. There are many Italians
who have come to it, and their old neighbors have moved out.
The only visitors that they have are their married children with
their families. Mrs. Gessell now and then visits her married
daughters, but Mr. Gessell does not accompany her.

The other families tell very much the same story: Week after
week with no other contacts than, for the man, the relief office,
with such sociability as might be found there, and perhaps the
corner stationery store or the saloon; for the woman, a visit from
a married daughter or a relative (if any of them lives in the
community). And such is apparently the social picture for the
past three or four years. It would seem that only the children
in the family and the deep economic anxiety have kept the hus-

band and the wife from realizing the full extent of their social isolation. There are a few exceptions among the families, but the above picture is true of the majority.

How much of this isolation is due to unemployment? We shall indicate below that the group under consideration has probably been always somewhat isolated, but there is no doubt that unemployment has played a major part in segregating the family from its customary social contacts.

Every family was asked, among other questions, whether unemployment had affected its social life. This question was answered affirmatively by 47 out of 59 families: unemployment has reduced the social life of the family. While in the past the family used to visit and entertain friends, they do so hardly at all at the present time.

Some attributed the change to the disloyalty of friends. Others stressed the economic aspect of social life. Social life costs money, and they simply could not afford it. Another group of families gave a still different explanation. They had, themselves, withdrawn from social life because they felt humiliated by their present status and inferior to most of their friends. Partly to protect themselves from being snubbed, partly to spare themselves the humiliation of comparisons, they had preferred to withdraw from all social life.

The families which felt that their friends had turned out to be disloyal fair-weather friends were very bitter on the subject.

An unemployed carpenter said, "As soon as you are out of the dough, your friends don't want to know you any more. They are afraid you will ask them for something. People on relief are black sheep. I used to make wine, and friends would drop around several times a week. It was nothing for me to give them a gallon to take away. I don't see anyone coming around now."

A former electrician said, "You don't have any friends unless you have got the dollar. If you have the dollar, you have got your true and loyal friend, and if you haven't got it, you're alone in the world."

A wife of a former glass worker said, "Our friends certainly did turn out to be fair-weather friends. Once they know you're down and out, they act as if you had a disease."

Another man said that the last few years had certainly made him wiser. He knows more about human nature than he ever did before. He had realized this: "People don't care if you die of starvation. They just turn around so as not to see it." He helped a lot of people when he was well off. Only the other day his little girl asked him where all those people were, and he said, "I don't know; I guess they've all moved to Boston." If he ever should have any more jobs to give out, they would all swarm around him.

A man who used to be a lineman said that he used to have a houseful of people every other day, but only one stood by through the hard times. This friend is on relief now, though he would remain a friend even if he were well off. The rest, and especially people he had given money to, had left him.

Not all of the families felt as much bitterness on the subject. Some explained the change in social life without blaming friends for disloyalty.

"Two people can't be friends when one is working and making money and the other is unemployed," said Mr. Cutter. "It just don't work out. The people who have the money don't want to stay at home and do nothing all the time. They want to go to a movie or take a ride, and they can't be expected to treat the other couple."

Mrs. Garland said the same thing. They had to stop seeing their friends because they couldn't do things together. And that referred not only to movies, and other outside recreation, but even to playing cards at home. Even though their friends played for very small stakes, the couple couldn't afford even that.

All of the families, with one or two exceptions, testified that social life is an expensive luxury. As one housewife put it, "The least you can offer is a cup of coffee and a piece of cake, and even that costs money." Many families said that they refused invitations because they could not reciprocate. They just told their friends not to invite them any more.

Finally, the third element in the decline in social life may be illustrated by an unemployed painter. "It may be all in my own head, but I feel inferior to the rest of the members of the church. They used to be my friends, but as it happened, they had better luck and kept their jobs. No, it isn't that they have snubbed me. I don't give them a chance to do that. I have learned to keep people at a distance so as not to get snubbed. They are well-to-do people and I feel out of it."

One woman says that their friends would love to have them over, but her husband refuses to go. She thinks he is ashamed of his present status. The rest of the men in the group are employed and start talking about their jobs, which makes her husband feel out of it.

Thus they explain the decline in informal social life. Very much the same explanation has been given by the families for the decline in the organized social life of the church and clubs. Sixteen who dropped church membership said that they had no money for the collection plate and didn't want to attend without some contribution. Furthermore, they felt "out of it." Women stressed lack of clothes. They would be objects of pity if they went to church in their shabby dresses. One woman said, "To tell you the truth, I still have one nice dress, but I cannot wear the same dress every Sunday." Still another woman is heartbroken about not being able to go to church because she cannot afford the carfare. Only one person gave other than economic reasons for dropping church membership. Mr. Scott, while he stopped attending church because he could not contribute, said that since unemployment he had lost faith in God, and even if he could afford joining the church, he would never take religion as seriously as he used to.

The clubs the men belonged to were largely lodges and unions. They dropped membership because they could not afford to pay the dues, and in one or two cases they dropped out because, being unemployed, they felt they were not on an equal footing with the other members. The few who had maintained memberships in unions, in lodges, and in political clubs, had done so in the hopes of maintaining contacts that might yield them a job.

The few exceptions to this picture of social isolation are interesting. The Page family did not lose their friends. Mr. Page was in great demand in the neighborhood for a card game. Besides, friends came over to play bridge, often bringing their own refreshments with them. "We were just saying," said Mrs. Page, "that we often have a better time than we used to have giving a formal party. You spend a lot of money on refreshments, and work a whole day to clean up and don't have as good a time as when people just drop in informally."

One man, an unemployed plumber, belonged to the Veterans of the Spanish War. In fact, all the social life he had was within the camp. He attended all the meetings and, as he said, they had been having quite a few funerals—a funeral every two or three months. Every member and his family had to attend the funerals. That is the only time he and his wife went out together. They did not visit any friends and never went to the movies.

Another exception is offered by two or three families who, in contrast to the rest, said that all of their friends were in the same boat as they were, so that there is no reason for them to feel humiliated by their poverty.

The absence of social life described above is true of the adults in the family. It is not true in the same degree of the children. Although changes in residence have in many cases disrupted old friendships, there is plenty of evidence of play groups and general social life in the case of the children. Nevertheless, the depression has affected them also. The children, even the youngest, are already so deeply conditioned to the adult valuations that they feel humiliated by the family's plight. It is sad to observe the shadow of humiliation under which the children live from day to day. This affects their relations with their playmates. Furthermore, lack of money affects social life in a more direct way. Their clothes are inadequate and they are unable to do things with their associates. The following cases are cited in illustration:

One girl, 15 years old, conceals from her friends that the family is on relief. She says that her father receives compensation (others say that their father is on a pension and still others say that the family had savings). The girl begs her father not to forget himself and mention relief when her friends are around. The child is in constant fear that the relief investigator will drop in while her friends are visiting her. She would never accept any clothes from the E.R.A. for fear her friends would recognize the source.

The little Baldwin boy is only 9 years old, but he refused to wear a jacket obtained from the Red Cross. This little boy explains to his playmates that he has no money for the movies or for candy because his parents believe that those things are not good for children.

One child refused to go to Sunday school without a penny to put into the collection plate. The children in another family, although missing the radio very much, do not go to the house of their friends to listen to the radio because they don't like to remind their friends that they do not have one. When this family finally acquired a radio, the children, according to their mother, were jubilant, and ran around telling one friend after another that they, *too*, had a radio.

There were three or four reported cases in which being on relief was used as a term of insult in a play group.

A 12-year-old girl told the following story: There are two girls, twins, in her school. Once the twins got into a fight with some girls, and the girls told them, "We know you're on relief," and the twins didn't go back to school for a long time after-wards. Another girl got into a fight with a playmate who accused her of being on relief. The girl retorted, "You're a good one to talk. You curse, and your mother curses and drinks, and she came home last night at two o'clock in the morning."

One girl, 15 years old, said that being on relief was the worst thing that ever happened in her life. The kids in school found out about it, and several of the mean ones made nasty remarks about it.

An 8-year-old child was asked by a group of playmates to go to a movie with them. The boy went in to ask his mother for money, but she didn't have a cent to give him. Ashamed to confess the truth, the boy returned and said, "Mother doesn't want me to go to movies, but she gave me some money for candy instead."

The adolescent children are, of course, still more depressed by the situation. Many of them conceal being on relief from their friends. Mary Kilpatrick said that she confessed to her best friend that she was on relief only after the girl came to her one day upset and crying because her family had to go on relief. To console her Mary told her that her own family was on relief.

The girl in the Holman family doesn't go out with boys because she would be ashamed to have them call for her. Their flat in the back of the house is so shabby that she is ashamed to invite even her girl friends there. Another girl does not invite her friends to her home because the family has no electric light.

Clothes are, of course, the main economic problem of the girls. The daughter of an unemployed automobile mechanic said that she was ashamed to go to school in the dress that she had worn every day for the whole winter. Not only the adolescent girls, but the younger ones also, have confessed that they stopped going to church because they did not have the proper clothes.

The economic problems of the boys were somewhat different. Few of them complained about the humiliation of shabby homes for, even if they went out with girls, the customary arrangement was for the boy to call at the girl's home. Furthermore, clothes did not play so much of a role. What they complained of was the lack of spending money.

Do poverty and the humiliation of being on relief throw the children of the unemployed together? There is only one report of a clique of school girls whose fathers are unemployed. On the whole, it seems that the neighborhood and personal congeniality play a more important role as the basis for children's friendships.

As one reflects upon the disruption of social ties following upon unemployment, it is sad to observe how tenuous these ties must have been. It is sad to think that in forty or fifty years of living, the man and the woman have not acquired friendships which would withstand the change in their socio-economic status.

One might ask, with reference to the adults, the same question that was asked with reference to the children: "Has there been a tendency for the unemployed to feel a consciousness of kind with regard to other unemployed?" That, apparently, has not been the case. Relatively few families said, "All our friends are in the same boat." It appears that the majority of the families were worse off than their friends. That is to say, for the socio-economic group to which they belonged relief was not the usual thing. If that is true, it would explain their strong reluctance to identify themselves with the families on relief. Indeed, many of them said that they didn't like to go to the relief office because of the "undesirable element" to be found there. Their deepest desire was to get off relief and return to normal life. It is significant that only two belonged to organizations of the unemployed.

The feeling of superiority toward the others on relief, and the repugnance toward identification with the "Niggers" and the "Wops," is one element that accounts for the lack of a sense of solidarity with the unemployed. Another was a kind of a competitive attitude. The others on relief were rivals, since they were competitors for the limited quantity of goods that the E.R.A. had to distribute. Very frequently the man or the woman would say, "If you ask for things politely and quietly, you don't get anything. The 'Niggers' come to the E.R.A. and make a big row, and they get more attention than we do."

It is interesting to speculate as to whether another group would show a similar decline in its social life as the result of unemployment. There is reason to suppose that different regional, nativity or religious groups would vary in this respect. It would seem that our group was particularly isolated even prior to unemployment. It had very few primary contacts. First of all the group consisted of residents of a large city rather than a small community. Thus, it had no ties to the neighborhood or to the community. Surely, a family in a small town would hardly lose all touch with the community life as a result of unemployment. It would still maintain some interest in the community institutions, if only from the point of view of the help that might be obtained from them: the Community Chest, or the Elks, or perhaps the "Lady Bountiful" of the community. The family would still be interested in the gossip of the community and maintain at least some contact with its residents.

In contrast to that, our group was an urban and a mobile group. Many were born outside the community and, furthermore, moved a good deal from neighborhood to neighborhood.

One might further speculate as to whether another religious group, particularly the Catholic one, would continue to maintain its contact with the church even during the depression.

Still another element in the social anatomy of our group is the relatively weak kinship ties as contrasted with a strongly patriarchal family. It is true that our families still maintain contact with relatives—the parents of husband and wife, sisters and brothers. Many of the families have secured both economic help and moral support from their relatives. Yet it is probable that an Italian or perhaps a Jewish group would have a more closely knit family unit. The responsibility toward kin, even distantly related, is probably greater among the strongly patriarchal groups. Among our families, very few made references to contacts with relatives, even as close as cousins, or to large family reunions.

Finally, to complete the picture of the families, we might repeat what was said about absence of class ties. Most men belong to unions, but as was already mentioned, had little class consciousness. The union was an employment agency, an instrument for improving working conditions without any emotional alignment or identification with its members.

These native-born Protestant skilled laborers thus appear to be a particularly individualistic group. Perhaps the social isolation at the present time is due precisely to the absence of organic social ties which characterized its existence even prior to unemployment.

One other factor may be mentioned, and that is the age of the couples. Most of them are over forty, and that may account partly for the absence of social life. The younger of the couples give indications of a somewhat more active social life even at the present time.

Whether the social isolation of the families made it harder or easier for them to bear the shock of the depression and unemployment, is not easy to say. From one point of view, it would seem that the families might have got moral support from close relations with some social group or individuals. Close relations would lessen their sense of being outcasts and would divert them from the incessant anxiety.

On the other hand, their very anonymity might have minimized the humiliation of the loss of status. The wife of a one-time automobile painter, for example, said that it would have been awful to have to go on relief in her home town where everyone knew her, but being on relief in this town did not matter. The retrenchments in standards of living might again be easier to bear since there are no friends to observe it. Some of the families who had few friends and whose lives centered around their own homes, never engaged in the usual competition in consumption and standards of living that goes on among friends. Their retrenchments were less painful because there were no comparisons to be made with friends, and because there were no witnesses, as it were, to their degradation.

THE EFFECT OF THE DEPRESSION ON SEX LIFE

The question arises as to how far the events of the depression changed the sex life of the couple. In many cases the interviewers found it difficult to approach the respondents on their sex life. Women were more able to question wives on this point, and men were more successful with husbands. Individuals differed very much in their ability to talk about their sex experiences.

The main question as to whether there has been any change at all during the depression in sex relations is answered affirmatively by most people. For 38 of the 59 cases information on sex was adequate. Of the 38, there were 16 that showed no change, while in 22 cases sex relations decreased in frequency, and in 4 of the 22 cases relations ceased altogether. No increases in frequency were noted, save in one case, in which the comment was made, "I think you want one another more when you're having hard luck than when everything is all right." It is safe then to say that sex life decreased, if it was affected at all.

In each case the respondent was asked for his or her reason for the change. Of the 22 families in which there was a decline, 8 claim that this came about for some reason not connected with the depression, such as ill health and the aging of the couple. But the remainder, 14, give some cause directly connected with the depression: fear of pregnancy was mentioned by 11 people, 2 said that relations were decreased because the wife lost respect for the husband because of the depression, and one claimed that "general anxiety" caused the decline.

It is evident that the alleged reasons may be merely convenient and socially acceptable excuses. It is hard to say what role the age of the couple played in the change. Comparison of the families in which there was no change in sex relations with those in which a decrease in frequency was observed shows that the latter are apt to be somewhat older.[19]

Turning to unemployment as a possible cause of the decrease in frequency, we note that various aspects have operated to produce it: fear of pregnancy due to lack of money to provide for the mother and child, changes in the wife's attitude towards her husband, changes in the husband's attitude due to his economic frustration, or general anxiety and nervousness because of economic insecurity.

Fear of pregnancy seems to be a specter haunting many of these families. Eleven of them gave this as the reason for the decline in sex relations. These people apparently felt that merely by decreasing frequency of relations they avoided the danger of having children. Many of them felt that families on relief had no right to have more children. Their comments were such as these:

"It is a crime for children to be born when the parents haven't got enough money to have them properly."

"It is a crime for a man to bring children into the world in our circumstances."

"A man hasn't got a right to a child unless he can support him."

Ignorance of birth control added to the fear of pregnancy. Of

[19]

TABLE 16

Present Age	Decline in Frequency	No Change	Total
Husband under 40...	7	8	15
Husband 40 and over.	15	8	23
Totals..........	22	16	38
Wife under 40.......	12	11	23
Wife 40 and over....	10	5	15
Totals..........	22	16	38

the 31 for whom the information is available, 14 families use birth control, and 17 do not. Even among those who claim to practice some form of contraception there is a good deal of ignorance concerning the medically accepted practices. Only one family indicated that they had ever heard of a birth-control clinic, and only one woman had had medical advice on contraception. For the most part these people relied on over-the-back-fence methods. At least three families had had children while using these haphazard methods, and the feeling of the unreliability of any birth control device was prevalent. It is interesting, however, that five families increased their use of birth control during the depression. One man told his story thus:

"I could have avoided my present status if I had taken precautions to have fewer children. Before the depression I never gave a thought to birth control. Both my wife and I were against it, and let the children come as they would. Had we been able to foresee the depression, we would have felt differently about it. I'm convinced now that birth control is a good thing."

Among those who did not practice any form of contraception the confusion with regard to birth control was even greater. Some believed it caused cancer, confused it with some harmful practice, or thought it meant a State-enforced limitation of the family. Other couples opposed it only on religious grounds as "interference with nature."

Decline in sex relations may also be due to the loss of respect and affection for the unemployed husband. In some cases the failure of the husband affected the wife's response to him as a lover. This was apparently the situation in the Garland family:

Mrs. Garland said that her husband seemed a bigger man to her when he was employed and was making good money. Of course his unemployment had changed her attitude towards him. "When a man cannot provide for the family and makes you worry so, you lose your love for him. A husband has to have four qualifications—first, second, and third he should be able to support the family, and fourth he should have personality." Her husband doesn't fulfill any of these qualifications. If she had the money she would probably get a divorce. Mrs. Garland said she did enjoy sex relations prior to unemployment, but does not now. She herself does not understand the reason for the change. It is not because she is afraid of pregnancy. Perhaps it is because she lost her love for her husband.

Mrs. Garland is 30 years old and her husband is 34. There are some indications that Mrs. Garland is carrying on an affair with another man.

It will be remembered that in the Patterson family the husband complains that he does not get as much affection since loss of employment—that when he tells his wife he wants love she just gets mad. In the Dorrance family, marital relations at the present time are very strained. The family has been on relief for four years. The wife says that they have not had any sexual contacts for over three years. She can't bear the thought of his touching her. She is quite sure he has been unfaithful to her during this time, but she doesn't care.

Decline in the wife's response towards the husband is, however, not the only explanation. The wife who never enjoyed sex relations found in the husband's unemployment a convenient way out.

Fear of pregnancy was a convenient rationalization for Mrs. Fucini. She said that she had never enjoyed sex, and since unemployment she has managed to talk her husband into believing that it is too dangerous for the family to take the risk of having another child and besides they were too old 'for that sort of thing, anyway. (Mr. Fucini is 45 and Mrs. Fucini is 36.) He suggested that she go to a birth-control clinic, but she refused.

In only one case was there evidence that the initiative for the decrease in sex contacts came from the husband himself. In this family the husband was a quiet, introverted man of 40 years. He felt deeply his inability to provide for the family. He said, "It is awful to be old and discarded at 40. A man is not a man without work." At first his wife blamed him for unemployment, but later she realized that it was not his fault. In fact, she began to console him and plead with him not to torment himself with his failure as a provider. At the time of the interview the wife showed resentment against the husband, but this resentment was directed not against unemployment, but against his personal changes—the fact that he was gloomy, depressed, and didn't pay any attention to his wife. She gave the interviewer to understand that there were no sex contacts because the husband thought that they were too old. It is possible that his failure and his wife's reproaches had affected his sexual potency. At any rate it was at his initiative that sexual contacts were discontinued.

APPENDIX

THE COMPOSITION OF THE FAMILIES

The composition of the fifty-nine families is presented in the following tables:

Nativity

Native-born parents 117
Foreign-born parents 1

Religion

Both spouses Protestant 44
Both spouses Catholic 4
Husband Protestant, wife Catholic.......... 9
Husband Catholic, wife Protestant.......... 2

Occupation of Husband Prior to Unemployment

Unskilled worker 8
Skilled worker 40
"White-collar" man 10
Owner of small business 1

Duration of Relief

1 year 4
2 years 12
3 years 14
4 years 21
5 years and over.......................... 8

Age of Husband

Under 30 years .... —
30 to 40 years............................ 21
40 to 50 years............................ 26
50 years and over......................... 12

Age of wife

Under 30 years........................... 3
30 to 40 years........................... 28
40 to 50 years........................... 19
50 years and over........................ 9

Age of Oldest Child

Under 10 years........................... 2
10 to 15 years........................... 22
15 to 20 years........................... 26
20 years and over........................ 9

DESCRIPTION OF DISCERNING

In discerning the causal relation between loss of authority and unemployment it must be made clear that we refer to the causal relation *in a particular case*. No generalization is attempted at this point as to how universally unemployment causes the change in question. Unemployment may be the cause of loss of authority in a particular case, but this in itself tells nothing of the relative tendency of unemployment to cause loss of authority. The case may be an exceptional one. Unemployment may be modified by numerous other factors to such an extent that it produces change under relatively exceptional conditions.

The procedure of discerning to be described below consists of the following steps:

1. Preliminary checking of the evidence to make it more specific and complete.
2. Checking the evidence for its consistency with other situations in the life of the respondent and, generally, with human reactions observed in similar situations.
3. Testing the possible alternative explanations of the change. The criteria in the third step are once again the relative consistency of one or another explanation with what is known of the life of the respondent and with general knowledge concerning human behavior in similar situations.

Before describing these various steps we shall present the *kinds of initial evidence* upon which discerning was based.

The initial statements of the respondents on changes during unemployment are of the following kinds:

a. *Statement of some sequence of events involving unemployment:* "Prior to unemployment the children used to go to my husband's church. Now they go with me to the Catholic Church." "My husband has been drinking since he has been unemployed." "I used to enjoy sex relations with my husband. I don't any more."

The above statements describe a sequence of events without any statement as to their causal relation. The change may refer to activity or to a state of mind, but there is no link between unemployment and the change.

b. *An interpretation of a sequence concerning another person:* "My wife lost respect for me because I failed as a provider." "My husband nags since unemployment because he has nothing to do all day."

c. *The person's confessed experience that unemployment caused a change:* Whenever a person reports not only a change but a personal motivation of the change, we have this kind of evidence. "I lost my love for my husband because he turned out to be a failure." "Unemployment made me lose faith in myself."

If the woman says, "We don't talk to each other as often as we used to," we have merely a sequence of unemployment and the change. If she adds, "because I am too disgusted with him to bother talking to him," then we have her experience as to the relation between unemployment and the change.

Many initial statements of the family involve a combination of the various kinds of evidence. "My wife used to be patient and kind, but now she nags so much that I cannot stand her any more and try to stay out of the house as much as I can." Such a statement includes both a report of a sequence of events (unemployment, wife nags more), and a testimony of a personal causal experience (nagging, caused man to stay away from home).

The first step of discerning is to subject the initial statements to a preliminary checking. There are two possible sources of error. The changes indicated may not have taken place, and they may not have been due to unemployment. Chapter 1 dealt with the first problem, but the emphasis there was upon uncovering changes rather than testing whether the alleged changes are or are not true. Although logically the procedure of discerning deals with the problem of the causal relation between unemployment and loss of authority or some other change, practically the two problems are interwoven and similar techniques are involved in the attempt to solve them.

The preliminary checking of the initial statements is achieved by a series of specifying questions to make the evidence more concrete and complete.

1. *Preliminary checking to make the evidence more specific and complete:* One kind of specifying question attempts to supplement sequences of unemployment and some change with statements of *experienced interconnection between the two.* This can be done by asking the respondents as to possible motives by which unemployment and the change in question could be linked more strongly.

It has been established that a man goes to church more often. Does he know why he goes more often now? Is it in the hope of making useful contacts or as a substitute for more expensive leisure time activities or because of increased need for religious consolation?

Similarly questions might be directed to find out what feature in unemployment appears to the respondent as the cause of the change.

It has been established that a man reads fewer books since he became unemployed. What in the unemployment situation has been the decisive causal feature of this decrease? Lack of money to pay his dues? Having no longer any access to the factory library? Spending all his time on job hunting? Losing interest in books because of worry?

Another kind of specifying question *is directed at a more detailed statement* of the link between unemployment and the change.

If a man says, "I used to be boss in the family, but now no one pays any attention to me," he is asked questions as to intermediate steps of this process. How did he recognize the fact? When did he first feel it? What did he do about it? How did members of the family react to it? And so on.

Submitting the original statements of the respondent to the above-described questioning may in some cases serve completely to eliminate alleged causal relations. If the reported sequence constituted a perfunctory answer, the respondent may not withstand the barrage of questions. In other cases, if we succeed in transforming statements of sequence into statements of experience of a causal relation, we have a more satisfactory kind of evidence. The woman who said that her children since her

husband's unemployment had been going to the Catholic Church
may confess that prior to unemployment she had had to acquiesce
to her husband's demands because otherwise he threatened to
withdraw his support from the family. Now she no longer
depends upon him for support and can do whatever she wants to.
This is considered a more adequate kind of evidence because
on the basis of our general observation of human behavior we
can understand it, we can perceive how unemployment has led
to the change.

The next check of the evidence for the causal relation between
unemployment and the change is an attempt to discover whether
the alleged condition is consistent with what we know of the life
of the respondent.

2. *Testing the consistency of the evidence:* Can the causal
relation between unemployment and the change be true? If one
factor is alleged to be the cause of some situation, then there
must be an association between the two phenomena. If we find
that one exists without the other, then the causal relation between them is not possible. Therefore, we look at the following
situations as tests of the validity of the causal explanation offered by the informant.

a. *The alleged casual factor was present in a different situation in the informant's life without producing the action or attitude claimed to be a result of it.*

ILLUSTRATIONS:

A wife testifies to a growth of conflict with her husband when she
began going out evenings. "I can't stand his reading a book all evening
without a word for me. I'd stay at home if he'd pay some attention to
me." Upon analysis it may appear, however, that he always was fond
of reading in the evening and never paid any more attention to her
than at the time she made the statement. The fact is that, for one
reason or another, she has refused to tolerate this situation since he has
been unemployed.

A woman says that it is natural that unemployment would make her
lose all respect for her husband, that a man who is a failure cannot
be respected; yet there is evidence that her unemployed brother still has
her respect and affection.

b. *The result has existed previously in the life of the informant
even when the alleged causal factor was absent.*

ILLUSTRATIONS:

The woman says that it is only unemployment that keeps the family
together, that they are very unhappy, and if it were not for their

poverty, they would break up the family. But the couple stayed together prior to unemployment when they could afford to maintain
separate homes, although evidence shows that relations were not better
then.

In addition to such logical tests, an attempt was made to
consider whether the statements of the respondents were psychologically consistent with the total evidence of the case. A woman
may deny that loss of earning ability has undermined her respect
for her husband. This statement may be inconsistent with what
is known about her values of life, her attitude towards her husband at the time of marriage, and her present behavior towards
him.

There were cases in which it was not possible to get the
respondent to state what the causal link was between unemployment and the change. A woman maintained that she did
not know why she ceased to enjoy sex relations with her husband
since unemployment. In this case and a few others, however,
the causal link between the two phenomena seemed highly
probable in spite of the fact that the respondent had not admitted it. Other information indicated that the failure of the
husband as a provider was a sharp blow to the wife. She was
disillusioned in the husband. His continuous presence at home
revealed to her, as she said, that he had no personality. She
blames him for unemployment and feels that a real man should
be able to provide for his family. Our general experience with
human reactions suggests that there might be a causal link
between these attitudes and the decline in this woman's response to her husband in the sexual sphere.

The usefulness of the above tests lies in revealing inconsistencies. They can show which of the alleged causal relations
between unemployment and the change are inconsistent. They
do not offer conclusive proof of their validity. Thus the wife
might testify to the increase in quarrels and attribute them to
the man's increased presence at home and interference with her
educational policies with the children. While, in terms of our
tests, this explanation may be consistent, it is possible that the
cause of the quarrels may be in a sphere which has nothing to
do with unemployment, perhaps, and the wife may prefer to
rationalize it in terms of the man's increased presence at home.
This leads us to another section of discerning: testing alternative explanations.

3. *Testing alternative explanations:* What other factors might

have accounted for the change in question? The more we know about the phenomena we are studying, the more hypotheses we can evolve as to the possible alternative interpretations of observed changes.

The problem of alternative explanations is particularly important in the consideration of parental relations. Father-child relations undergo changes in the normal course of development. More than that, the changes that take place are in the direction of the emancipation of the child from the father's authority. Adolescence is likely to bring about increased conflict and a more or less conscious struggle of the child for self-determination. In other words, coincident with unemployment there has been going on a process of growth. How can we decide whether the loss of authority is due to unemployment or to the growth of the child? As a matter of fact, we can seldom be sure that change in authority would not have occurred had it not been for unemployment. All we can say is that unemployment has been, or has not been, a contributory factor. It is judged to be a contributory factor under three conditions:

a. If the conflict which precipitated loss of control was an aspect of unemployment.
b. If the father felt that unemployment undermined his power in dealing with the child.
c. If the child explicitly utilized unemployment in his struggle for emancipation.

Cases in which loss of authority is observed, but in which the conditions, (a), (b), and (c) do not exist, we consider not affected by unemployment. There were 4 cases in which growth of conflict and some loss of the father's control was observed, but the change was to all appearances completely unrelated to unemployment.

Certain other alternative hypotheses with regard to changes in parent-child relations may be stated as follows:

a. *How may a possible change in folkways affect the problem?* Since times have changed, children may perhaps demand greater freedom from regulation.
b. *Has aging of parents anything to do with the change being studied?* Perhaps they are less patient and more irritable with the younger children, which in turn causes conflict. All such problems should, if possible, be tested according to the directions indicated above.

Even if there are no older children for purposes of comparison, the informant should be asked whether the mere fact of the children's growing older may not offer a complete explanation of the change. Can he be sure that the disciplinary problems would not have arisen had there been no depression?

c. *How do differences in personalities of the children affect the problem?* It may be that the differences between the older and the younger children are the result, not of the depression, but of differences in personalities—such as the fact that the younger ones may be more stubborn or rebellious.

To summarize, we have assumed that unemployment caused a particular change when:

a. The informant has answered satisfactorily the specifying questions.
b. No inconsistency has been observed between the explanation in the light of other evidence in his life.
c. Apparently no other factors were present to explain the change.

The procedure of discerning will be briefly illustrated as it was applied to two cases. We shall illustrate only the reasoning involved in stages two and three, omitting the preliminary set of questions designed to get as concrete and complete a statement of changes as possible.

Brief Illustrations of Discerning

CASE 1

Evidence of unemployment being the cause of loss of authority.

1. Statement of wife that she is dissatisfied with her husband because of his unemployment.
2. Statement of the husband that there are more marital conflicts since unemployment.
3. Statements of both that the conflicts consist in the wife's blaming her husband for hardships.
4. Change in the manner in which the wife treats the husband. The wife used to control her dissatisfactions with her husband. She is freer in expressing her dissatisfactions now.

On the basis of other evidence in the case it appears that the respondents are sincere and intelligent. Therefore we accept their testimony as to the increase in conflict.

Internal consistency and alternative explanations: As to the second problem, "Is the conflict due to unemployment?" we accept the contents of the conflict as strong evidence of the causal link. They fight over his inability to find work. This, however, is no final proof. We know that some quarrels are frequently symbolic of underlying conflicts—that the apparent cause of the discussion is not the real one. It is possible that the other changes in the relations of the couple that have nothing to do with unemployment caused the growth of conflict, and that both of them prefer to rationalize this other conflict in terms of his inability to find work.

Suppose his mother came to live in the city, and the wife became very jealous of her, and resented the mother-son relations. Suppose that because of her upbringing she considers filial obligations as holy, and doesn't dare to say anything about it. She may show her irritation by picking on his unemployment, while under ordinary circumstances she would have absolved him from guilt.

If this other real conflict is a result of unemployment, we can, of course, still relate the phenomena to unemployment. But if we do not know what this other conflict may be, we cannot do so. What did we do to elicit the hidden conflicts? We went through the daily routine of life. If the other conflict had been a conscious one, we might have got it through our questioning; but if it was suppressed, it is doubtful that we would have uncovered it. For the conflict to have eluded us we must assume further that it was suppressed and done so by both respondents, which is a more remote possibility.

To summarize: We have decided that unemployment caused a change in this particular case because we had a reasonable explanation of the manner in which unemployment has caused it together with an absence of any hint of other explanations.

CASE 2

Evidence of unemployment being the cause of loss of authority

1. The husband's experience that unemployment caused a general change in the wife's sentiments: "I don't get as much love since I am unemployed."

2. The wife's experience that changes in husband irritate her: "I am disgusted with the way he has changed since unemployment."
3. Statement of both husband and wife that the wife is going out more often without the husband because he is too sour and depressed to want to go out.
4. Testimony as to sequences of events, closer relations between wife and daughters since unemployment, changes in the behavior of the husband.

The above testimony was checked for agreement in the three interviews.

Internal consistency and alternative explanations: There are two possible sources of error in the above testimony: (a) The alleged changes may not have occurred at all; (b) the change may have occurred for some other reason than unemployment. When the man says he does not get as much affection because of his unemployment, we cannot accept his statement uncritically. Perhaps he was never loved by the wife, and he is glad to attribute the cause to unemployment. Now he can blame his wife for being mercenary and say, "Love flies out the window when money goes." When the wife says that she is disgusted with her husband for his unemployment, it is possible that she also prefers to attribute to unemployment attitudes which have their source elsewhere. It is possible that she has always been dissatisfied with her husband.

On the other hand, it is possible that the changes have occurred but that their reason lies not in unemployment but elsewhere. The husband may say that the reason for his wife's change in sentiments is his unemployment. Perhaps he has become less adequate as a lover for various reasons, and the wife's change of sentiment is a reaction to it. It is also possible that while she says she is disgusted with him because of changes in his personality, the truth may lie elsewhere. Such are the possible sources of error.

We have accepted, however, the original statements because the total interviews contained material in support of them.

There is evidence that his personality changed as a result of unemployment. He describes the feelings of uselessness, restlessness, and humiliation. The daughter whose attitude towards her father is favorable confirms that he has changed for the worse. All three members of the family confirm the fact that the mother spends more time with the daughter, which means less time with the husband. She does more things together with the daughter, leaving the husband alone evening after evening. We thus infer that she has less time for her husband and less chance for affection and companionship.

Furthermore, the study of predepression marital relations shows that the wife never loved her husband, but appears to be the kind of woman who would restrain her feelings in the interests of economic security. In other words, it seems reasonable that she might withdraw her semblance of affection when she became economically free of her husband.

We have scrutinized the evidence for a possible cause of the observed changes other than unemployment but found no hint of other factors.

In summary, it may be said that it was decided to consider that the change in the wife's sentiments has actually taken place. The change was attributed to unemployment because we found reasonable connection with unemployment in the absence of any suggestion of alternative explanations.

In the study of marital relations, we found only one case in which loss of the husband's authority was apparently unrelated to unemployment. There were four cases in parental relations in which the loss of authority was attributed to other factors than unemployment.

In the T. family the only indication of loss of authority is the wife's statement:

"But I think lately I am sticking up for my rights a little more than before. I told Mr. T. what I thought of his throwing the children out of the house. He did it anyway, but I told him what I thought of it. I argue more with Mr. T. about his strictness with the children. Mr. T. thinks that I have changed. He told me just the other day that he thinks I have changed a good deal. I don't notice it. I don't even know what he has in mind. No, I don't think he means that I am sticking up for my rights. I don't know what he means."

But there is no indication that that change, whatever its significance, has anything to do with unemployment. Mrs. T. doesn't blame her husband in the slightest for his unemployment. She doesn't feel that his unemployment reduces his claims upon the family. There are indications that she still admires Mr. T. and is devoted to him. She insists that it is the final fight with the children that convinced her that Mr. T.'s policy with the children does not work well. It is possible that she was sure of it before, but the outcome of the final fight with the children gave her courage to express herself.

The possible source of error in this interpretation is the following: Mrs. T. may prefer to attribute to Mr. T.'s educational policy what, in reality, is due to unemployment. Perhaps it is Mr. T.'s unemployment that diminished her awe of him. She realized that he was not infallible. However, there just doesn't seem to be any indication of that. It was not possible to arouse any emotion in Mrs. T. with regard to unemployment and the depression, while tears appeared in her eyes when parental relations were discussed. The interview with Mr. T. confirmed the impression that unemployment is as yet not a painful problem in marital relations.

CONCLUSIVENESS OF DISCERNING

Discerning whether or not unemployment was the cause of changes was not equally conclusive in all cases. In a general way the conclusiveness depends upon two conditions: (a) The nature of the causal connection between unemployment and the change in the particular case; and (b) completeness of available evidence. We shall discuss them briefly:

1. *The nature of causal connection between unemployment and the change.*

a. Is unemployment a sudden break or is it gradual? Discerning is easier when unemployment is a sudden change. First, if unemployment came about gradually, the change is less dramatic, and it is harder for the informant to perceive changes that are due to it; and secondly, it is somewhat harder for the interviewer to check the explanation.

Let us take two situations: A prosperous family suddenly losing its wealth as compared with another family becoming gradually impoverished. It is clear that in the first case the family will have a more vivid picture of the change, and will be able to realize more clearly what changes have occurred as a result of the loss of wealth. The advantage for the interviewer will be a similar one. He will have a clear-cut comparison, and will be able to check more easily the statements of the members of the family.

b. Is the change gradual or sudden? If the change is gradual it is harder for the informant to perceive it, and to perceive its connection with unemployment. Furthermore, it is harder to interpret it because other factors had a chance to intervene. This change may be a joint product of unemployment and other factors.

c. How direct is the relation between unemployment and the change? The more immediate the relation, the easier it is to discern it. If the relation is intermediate, there are more sources of error both in the informant's perceiving the relation and in the interviewer's checking of it. If the woman says, "Since unemployment my husband has been mean to the children; they resent it and give me more trouble, and I hate him for it," there are more steps that must be checked than if she had said, "Since unemployment we quarrel over relief."

d. The degree to which a single individual was actively implied in the change. If the change constituted a conscious decision which an individual had to make himself, the discernibleness of unemployment as a cause of this decision might be greater than if it were something which happened to the individual.

2. *The completeness of available evidence.*

a. How intelligent is the informant in analyzing sequences? Does he leave the interviewer with the statement: Husband started to drink after unemployment; or, is he analytical enough to explain the motives and interpret experience?

b. Is the informant frank, or is he on guard? Does he answer in cultural stereotypes, or confess socially disapproved attitudes?

c. Is there danger of a bias, conscious or unconscious, either in the direction of stressing or denying that unemployment is a cause of the change?

d. Are there inconsistencies and contradictions within the interview, or between the interviews?

THE CRITERIA OF AUTHORITY TYPES

The criteria of the wife's attitude are set forth first, followed by the discussion of the criteria of dominance.

Instrumental was defined as follows: Wife has no love or admiration for her husband. Such authority as he has is accorded to him by the wife on instrumental grounds, largely as a price for the economic and social security of marriage. Antagonistic attitudes are always present, varying from contempt to hatred. There may or may not be fear of husband.

Primary: Wife's attitude characterized by love for the husband and respect. In some cases love may be dominant without profound admiration, or, indeed, any admiration for the husband. Utilitarian elements may exist, but presence of love and admiration distinguishes the primary attitude from instrumental. On the other hand, absence of areas of major conflict, absence of serious dissatisfaction with the husband and of resentment against him distinguish it from mixed authority. Some families with conflict were included in the primary group, but only since this conflict was the outcome of the ambivalence of love, as in case of "emotional bondage."

Mixed: Attitude of wife has features of both primary and instrumental authority.

Since it is the predepression attitudes of the wife that are to be determined, it is especially important to avoid confusing them with the present attitudes. Parts of the questionnaire dealing with the circumstances of marriage bear directly upon predepression sentiments. We can ascertain through direct questioning and through inference whether or not the wife was in love with her husband at time of marriage, or whether, on the other hand, the utilitarian motive predominated at that time. The husband is questioned also as to circumstances of marriage, which serves as a check upon the wife's interview.

But the main source of information as to the wife's attitude comes from the study of the present situation, checked by rigid questioning with regard to possible changes. When we get evidence of an attitude, we ask whether or not change has occurred, and if the result is negative, we assume that the attitude existed prior to the depression.

There are then two patterns of evidence: (1) Evidence of love for husband at time of marriage with further evidence that no changes have occurred up to the time of unemployment; (2) Love for husband at the present time, with evidence that this does not reflect any changes since unemployment. Both of these patterns were usually utilized in every case.

Such evidence as the following was considered proof of primary authority, that is, of love or admiration. Direct statement of husband and wife or children: "They're crazy about each other. They're in love—as much in love as when first married." Child says, "Daddy kisses mother all the time." "Our love lasted through the bearing of 13 children." The wife said she would not leave husband no matter what happened; in fact she would rather be parted from her children than her husband, if that should be necessary. She doesn't regret marrying the particular husband, and would do it over again. She defines a good husband by saying, "Like my own husband." Wife likes to talk to husband because he is "so sweet." Husband says, "If it weren't for my wife's devotion, I don't know what I would have done during the depression. No man would want a better wife. We are still like sweethearts. I would rather spend an evening with her than do anything else."

These direct expressions of a wife's attitude were checked against husband's statements and other evidence of the case, and accepted only if not contradicted by all of the other evidence.

In addition to direct statements, inferences were made from the following situations: Wife defends husband against her relatives. Wife expresses solicitude about husband's well-being, not letting him go out to look for work when the weather is bad. Wife tries to distract husband from worrying.

In the case of *instrumental authority* it is more difficult to infer the past from the present. If the woman says that she is very much in love with her husband at present, and after questioning maintains that there have been no changes in relations in recent years, it is possible to accept her statement without much doubt, especially when checked against statements of the other members of the family. The situation with instrumental authority is different. A woman is irritated or disgusted with her husband. This would give her some predisposition to view the past through the prism of her present attitude. Some, perhaps, might idealize the past, while others darken it. That is why, when we came across resentment for the husband at the present time, we spent much more time on trying to reconstruct the predepression situation, not only at time of marriage, but also at later stages of marriage, and up to the depression.

Such evidence as the following was considered as constituting instrumental authority: "Yes, it was love at first sight, but love can go very quickly." "I was sorry I got married a couple of months afterwards." "No, I had few suitors, worse luck. I didn't have a chance. My parents kept me in very strictly, so, I fell for the first boy I went out with." "I would never have gotten married so young if it weren't for my parents' strictness, and I surely am sorry for it." "Women should look up to their husbands, but I never could. When I got married I thought I could change him, teach him how to read, and get him interested in educational things. But I soon saw it was no use." "My husband could never keep a job. He is lazy." "Unemployment has nothing to do with our state, because it wasn't any better prior to unemployment. He was never a good provider, and that was a big disappointment to me." "The only reason I stayed was for the children." "He spent most of his weekly pay in the saloon, but there was nothing I could say about it, because he was so mean and cruel to me and the children."

The distinction between instrumental authority and primary authority with antagonistic sentiments was made on the evidence in the whole case. Thus, in one case, husband was unfaithful to wife, and wife criticized him bitterly, but added, "and the worst of it is, I guess I still love him." The woman expressed the general opinion that living with a man, no matter how bad he is, makes the woman his slave.

Cases of *mixed authority* were cases that did not fall into either of the above categories because they had elements of both. There are two border lines to define: How antagonistic must the attitude be to be called instrumental rather than mixed, and how favorable must it be to be called primary rather than mixed.

The line between primary and mixed is defined by the presence or absence of antagonistic feelings towards the husband. There is one exception to this rule. Cases of personal bondage are clearly cases in which, in spite of strong physical and emotional attachment to the husband, there exist antagonism and conflict with him. Such cases were, nevertheless, put into the primary category. However much antagonism might exist, the grounds of subordination to the man were strictly primary rather than instrumental.

Another distinction between primary and mixed lies in the presence or absence of strong fear of the husband. Whenever there was some indication of fear of the husband as a ground of authority, the case was put in the mixed category. Evidence of fear might come from the wife's confession. The wife in one case says that she cannot restrain her husband's violence with the children because she herself is afraid of him when he is angry. In another, the husband beats his wife, and fear of his violence is a factor in her submission. In two other cases fear takes subtler forms. In both cases the husbands have tempers. The apprehension and anxiety that these wives show when their husbands are displeased, have all the earmarks of fear.

The detection of fear was not always possible. We may have succeeded in discovering it only in cases of violent husbands, or in families with some marital conflict. It is possible that in the cases which we classed under primary authority there may be wives whose dependence upon a superior and domineering man, although outwardly voluntary and without conflict, has an element of fear in it. But if the hostility towards the husband which is probably an inevitable correlate of fear was repressed, if the husband did not give any evidence of utilizing fear as a means of domination, the case would remain in the class of primary authority.

We have included as primary authority some cases in which we had little evidence of love, but rather a peaceful habituation. That is to say, an attenuated kind of affection was grouped as primary authority provided there was no antagonistic feeling. There might be some irritation, but the kind of which the wife would say, "Oh, once in a while he gets on my nerves, but not very often, and it doesn't amount to anything." In such cases the interview would not reveal any anger against the husband in any particular respect, or any criticism of the husband. The admiration may be mild. The woman might say, "He is a good man. I might have done worse." But she will not name any major deficiencies in the husband that are a source of irritation.

The dividing line between instrumental and mixed is the absence of any indication of love and admiration. In one case which was put in the mixed group, the woman is sorry she ever married the man because he is not her kind, but she realizes that he is her superior and there are indications that she admires him in a way. In another case, there is a good deal of conflict. The wife is sorry she married young. He used to drink a good deal, but still she might have wanted to marry the same man, though later in life; and he used to be a good provider; sometimes she thinks she is as fond of him as most wives are of their husbands.

Criteria of Dominance

Categories used: (a) Husband dominant, (b) wife dominant, (c) balance of power.

a. *Husband dominant:* Husband's dominance was judged on the basis of such evidence as the following: *Control of spheres;* husband decides major problems in the lives of the couple— residence, children's vacations, leisure-time interests—conflicts are decided in the husband's favor. In one case, the husband controlled the budgeting of the limited resources; the wife had different ideas about how it should be done, but submitted to him to keep peace in the family.

Control must be studied in its psychological context rather than in its merely formal aspects. In one case, for example, the husband assumed complete management of money during the depression, but it would hardly be accurate to say there was a gain in authority; in fact, it was a defeat for the husband. The wife had always wanted him to take charge of money matters; she felt it was the man's job and didn't want to be bothered with it. Only after her husband's unemployment, however, was she able to gain a victory over him with regard to it.

If there are no conflicts, it is more difficult to ascertain dominance. One may discover it by finding that the submissive spouse has other desires and interests in the particular situation, or that the initiative for a decision always comes from the other. An interesting case is presented by the following situation. Imagine a wife who prefers a dependent role, who dislikes taking initiative. The husband is of the same type. Paradoxically the struggle for authority is a struggle for submission. The defeated one is to assume authority. The woman mentioned above, who forced her husband to assume complete management of the family's financial affairs, is a case in point. One would consider it a defeat for the husband if one saw its origin. If, on the other hand, one entered the situation after the husband has become accustomed to the control of money, one would find the wife always asking him for money. We should find him making the major decisions. We should certainly be apt to say that he has the authority, at least in this sphere. If he is thoroughly accommodated to it, and no longer resents it, then perhaps he does have the authority, although originally assumed against his will. If, on the other hand, he still chafes under it, then we should find some manifestation of such an attitude and consider control of money merely an execution of his wife's will.

The problem of ranking the various spheres is a complicated one. Marital relations do not always present a simple authoritarian pattern of submission or balance of power in all spheres. One spouse may be submissive in some and dominant in others. Sometimes the ranking of the spheres is quite simple. If the wife's jurisdiction is over such matters as whether the children wear rubbers when they leave in the morning, and the husband's over such matters as church, education, or the vocational interests of the children, their relative roles are obvious. It is not always as simple, however. A simple, unintellectual woman may accept her husband's domination in intellectual affairs while, in turn, dominating his emotional and practical life. Cases in which both husband and wife dominate different spheres of equal significance, we call balance of power cases.

So much for control of spheres as evidence of dominance.

Other evidence on the basis of which husband was judged to be dominant: (1) Wife looks up to husband and consults him before expressing an opinion. This is accepted as evidence of his domination only in the absence of contradictory evidence, as, for example, her domination of certain spheres; (2) Wife afraid of husband, for example, conceals matters that arouse his anger; (3) Wife dependent upon husband, saying that without him she would be lost. This, again, is evidence of his dominance only if there is no conflicting testimony as to her control of other spheres.

The above evidence may come from direct statements of experience such as statement of wife, "I am not hard to please; whatever he says goes." Or, "He is boss when it comes to the children; when I cannot do anything with them I always call him in." On the other hand, some evidence is drawn from observation of activities and situations without the informant's interpretation of them: behavior of the couple during the interview, or description of a particular situation.

b. *Wife dominant:* Wife dominance was ascertained on the basis of similar evidence.

c. *Balance of power:* Cases in which there is no dominance of either spouse present three possibilities: (1) One of the spouses may be dominant, but the interviewer may have been unable to detect it; (2) The spouses have such similarity of interests that the authority of neither spouse is put to the test, because both want the same things. It is hard to imagine that the entire marital relationship may present such identity of interests; (3) The spouses have equal power.

Equality of power within marital relations may mean several things: The family may be equalitarian in the sense of joint decisions on all family matters. In another case there may be continuous conflict with no clear victory for either spouse. A wife may not be able to force her husband to give up drinking. He, on the other hand, may not have any greater power of influencing her and forcing her to conform to his wishes.

Still another variety would appear under the balance-of-power category. Husband and wife may dominate very different spheres, as, for example, the case of an unintellectual woman admiring her husband for his intellect and yet dominating his practical life. This relation is, of course, quite different from the one in an equalitarian family. Thus, the term "balance of power" is a kind of a quantitative expression that does not reveal qualitative differences within the category.

ANALYSIS OF DUPLICATE INTERVIEWS

In order to test the reliability of the questionnaire an interesting experiment was conducted in the course of the study. Families originally studied by one member of the staff were reinterviewed by another four months after the first interview. The second interviewer had not read the original interview. The only information concerning the family that he had had prior to the second interview was the background information available for each case from the relief records.

The second interviewer took a letter to the family asking for the privilege of another interview. The explanation given was that the study required supplementary information. The second interview was paid for at the same rate as the first. Five such duplicate interviews were obtained.

The five sets of interviews were analyzed for similarities and discrepancies. The analysis incidentally was done not by the interviewers but by a person especially engaged for the purpose. Duplicating the interviews bears upon the reliability of the questionnaire more than upon its validity. The mere fact that the instrument has yielded similar conclusions with its repeated use does not in itself prove the validity of the questionnaire. It may be, for example, that the respondent has consistently misrepresented the situation on both occasions, that on both occasions the questionnaire has failed to detect subtle changes in attitudes or that some of our purported tests of authority do not really reveal what they were intended to show.

In reading the duplicate interviews one is struck first of all by their remarkable similarity to the original interviews. The two sets of interviews agree with regard to the essential points. Both interviews yielded identical conclusions on the central problems; that is, on the kind of marital and parental relations prior to unemployment and the presence or absence of deterioration in the man's authority. The information given by the wife and the husband in the duplicate interview agreed generally with that supplied in the first with regard to the following problems:

The specific role of each parent in bringing up the children, changes in the husband's role due to the depression, attitude toward husband at time of marriage and major changes in marital life before the depression, relative amount of satisfaction with husband before the depression, relative dominance of husband

and wife in various spheres of marital relations before and after the depression, the reactions of each to changes and so on.

Because of the similarity between the duplicate and original interviews their comparison can be best presented by setting forth discrepancies rather than identical information appearing in both interviews.

The discrepancies between the two sets of interviews fall into two groups. Some discrepancies are relatively unimportant from the point of view of the purpose of the duplicate interviews, as, for example, those which appear because questions asked in one interview were not asked in the other.

Similarly, some differences are due to changes in the life of the family. In one case the younger child had left school and obtained a job. He had started going around with "bad company" which worried the father a great deal. The father's relationship with the boy had changed, which changed most of the information concerning the parent-child relations.

Other discrepancies are more important for the problem at hand. One major discrepancy gives a different picture of the preunemployment marital relations. To the first interviewer the wife said that she had felt disillusioned about her husband even prior to unemployment. He had no "push," and she had turned down some fine chances to marry other men and has always regretted it. To the second interviewer the picture, while not that of a happy family, was not nearly so bad. She said that she always considered her husband a go-getter, and that she was satisfied with his success at selling insurance before the depression. However, to the second interviewer she also admitted that they had had arguments about money before, but that their arguments were much worse during the depression.

Minor discrepancies are much more frequent. The interviews disagree with regard to predepression earnings, details of occupational history, details of regulation in various spheres of children's lives, what the family experienced as the greatest hardship of unemployment, and so on. Generally the information concerning specific behavior—such as movie attendance, use of the radio, social life—shows greater similarity than answers with regard to attitudes.

We have selected for illustration two sets of interviews which show the greatest number of discrepancies, one with regard to parental relations, another with regard to marital relations.

The Mother's Interviews

School

First: The father helps more with the homework because she is usually busy around the house.

Second: They do not come to either parent for aid in their schoolwork. (They used to go to their father.) This is not because they lost respect for their father since unemployment, but because the parents are not qualified to help with advanced studies.

Health

First: The father is the one who is strict about when the children shall come in or go out.

Second: She does not know which one imposed this regulation.

Play and Associates

First: The children never go anywhere without asking their mother.

Second: Mother makes no restrictions as to where the children should play. Believes that children should have more independence.

Church

First: They always took rides on Sunday, but the children went to Sunday school first.

Second: They always took rides on Sunday, and the children missed Sunday school and church.

Money

No differences.

Radio, Movies, and Other Hobbies

First: The boys and girls read everything they can get their hands on, in fact this is a major activity.

Second: The boys and girls have no hobbies.

Occupational Plans

First: They will all take the commercial course in high school and try to get office jobs with some big company like the Prudential and work up.

Second: The children have never spoken to parents about their educational plans. Mother knows they would be ashamed to work in a factory.

Father and Children

First: Father is still the big boss when he comes home, though he doesn't bother much with the children. Perhaps they don't mind him as well, but that is because he has drawn into himself more and is pretty discouraged.

Second: Father has lost no control over the children. He is more irritable, but tries not to have the children know it. When he is that way he usually goes into a corner by himself and doesn't bother anyone, so that the children are not affected by his irritability.

Children and the Depression

First: The girls suffer because of poverty. They want clothes and dances and movies and all the things a young person should have. They're always complaining about it. But the mother has never heard a word of reproach to either father or mother.

Second: The children do not seem to mind the fact that the father does not have much money to spend on them, and they have never said anything about it to either parent. Of course, they might say something in a joking way, but they never mean anything by it.

Supervision of the Children

First: She slaps one or all of the three smallest children almost every day. Spanks the others about once a month.

Second: She does not believe in hitting the children, but since the depression she is nervous, and when they make a good deal of noise, she cannot help herself and she slaps them, and then always regrets it later.

The father's interviews on parental relations also had certain discrepancies. Examples of them follow:

The Father's Interviews

Supervision

First: He occasionally loses his temper and then he hits the boys very hard, but not the girls.

Second: Neither father nor mother ever hit any of the children.

School

None.

Health

None.

Play and Associates

First: He has always been able to guide the children's choice of friends simply by talking to them about the right kind.

Second: He has told the children not to play with certain children and they always obey him.

Radio, Movies, and Other Hobbies

None.

Occupational Plans

None.

Money

First: The boys brought home their pay checks to him.

Second: If the boys need money, they go to their mother for it. She keeps the money, and it is natural that they should go to her.

Father and Children

First: It isn't good for the children to see their father around the house all day. He gets irritated, and it is, "Don't do this" and "Don't do that" all day long.

Second: He does not think his presence at home has made much difference in his relation with his children.

Children and Depression

First: Lack of clothing, inadequate food, and lack of spending money, have been the hardest things on the boys.

Second: Boy of twenty-one would have gone through school, but there is nothing else they especially miss. He doesn't think the depression has affected the children in any special way.

It is interesting also to compare the wives' and husband's interviews for similar minor discrepancies on marital relations.

Wife's Interviews

Details of Courtship

First: She went with her husband only a few months before marriage.

Second: She knew her husband one and a half years before marrying him.

First: She married when she was 18 and he was 20.

Second: She married when she was 17 and he was 20.

Occupational History

First: Husband was working as an electrician when she married him.

Second: Husband was in the Navy when she went with him, and went into a drug concern immediately after marriage.

Attitude of Parents

First: Her parents figured she was old enough to know her mind and were glad to have her marry so the children would have a home.

Second: Parents did not object, although they believed her husband was a very quiet individual, but only told her this once and told her to do whatever she wanted to.

Change in husband due to the depression

First: Husband has not revealed any new qualities, but, if anything, is quieter and keeps more to himself.

Second: Husband has not revealed any new qualities, except that he is a little more irritable.

Wife's present reaction to marriage

First: Yes, she believes that she would have married her present husband even if she could have been able to anticipate the present conditions.

Second: If she had known the present would be as it is, she would have thought a second time about marrying him.

There are similar discrepancies in the husband's interviews:

Husband's Interviews

Salary

First: Before the depression he earned $60 a week.

Second: Before the depression he earned $75 a week.

In-Laws

First: They see their in-laws seldom. He and his wife are not on very good terms with his sister-in-law, but she does a lot for the children.

Second: Family never bothered with in-law trouble. He and his wife's family get along very well. In fact, he could get along with anyone.

Leisure time activities

First: There is never a lack of enough people to get up a card game. That is their usual form of entertainment.

Second: He usually plays cards with the rest of the family. He doesn't like to, but only does it to be agreeable.

Hardest part of Unemployment

First: The hardest part of unemployment is worry about the future, and the feeling that he is in a rut.

Second: The hardest part of unemployment is the constant worry about the family's economic needs.

If he had a lot of money

First: He would do a lot of drawing and improve himself and study.

Second: He would see that all his children had a good education. He would first provide handsomely for his family and then he would try to help those who had not been so fortunate as he had been.

The question now arises: what is the reason for such discrepancies as do exist?

The sex, personality, and skill of the interviewer must in part account for variation in the answers. With regard to sex relations women were able to interview wives more candidly than were the men, while the men were able to get more information from their own sex. But in general the difference in rapport due to sex of the interviewer does not always work in the same direction. One man said that he was ashamed to admit to a woman that he was on relief, while he admitted it to the second interviewer who was a man. We cannot say, however, that the men bragged to the women interviewers because there was one case in which the man was much more candid to the woman interviewer. He exaggerated his earnings before the depression to the man interviewer. It would seem that the differences in the skill and personality of the interviewer were more important than differences in sex in establishing rapport with the respondent.

Other discrepancies in the interviews were due to the respondents. Some were due to the fact that the respondents remembered the first interview and in the duplicate interview gave information to shield themselves. The questionnaire was constructed in such a manner that direct questions concerning attitude came after the indirect ones in such a way the respondents in the first interview were frequently led into admitting attitudes or practices before realizing the full import of their confessions. At the time of the second interview the respondents knew enough of the trend of the interview to be able to protect themselves. Even when certain admissions were made, there was a tendency to rationalize and justify these practices. Thus on page 156 the woman who confessed slapping her children in the first interview said in the second that she didn't believe in hitting the children; that sometimes she cannot help herself, but always regrets it. The father denied it completely in the second interview. On the same page there is a similar discrepancy. In the first interview the mother said that the children were always complaining about the depression. In the second interview they don't complain to either parent.

While the cause of discrepancies just described lies in deliberate attempts of the respondents to put themselves in as good a light as possible and correct the impression given in the first interview, there are other differences which are probably unintentional. Some of the questions call for generalizations on the part of the respondents. They are expected to think concerning a number of specific events and generalize as to either their relative importance or their implications for family relations. In many cases it was the first time that they were forced to think about the problem. When the situation is not extreme, it may well happen that the respondent arrives at different conclusions.

Even such a question as "Has your husband become more irritable?" requires a generalization with regard to a number of specific instances of the husband's behavior at the present time and in the past. Similarly such questions as "What about unemployment was hardest on the family?" may again be answered differently from time to time if one or another aspect of the depression is especially oppressive. The mood of the moment, the occurrences immediately preceding the interview—such as a quarrel with the husband—may determine the answer. It is to such causes that we must attribute certain differences. One man said that the hardest thing about the depression was worry about his family, while in his second interview he said that having too much time on his hands was the main worry. In view of these difficulties it is remarkable that the discrepancies were as infrequent as they were.

To summarize, it may be said that perhaps the greatest source of the discrepancies lies in the questions calling for generalizations on the part of respondents. When a question involves a comparison of a number of specific events and when the situations are not clear-cut, it may be a matter of chance as to which of several alternatives is picked out at a given time. The character of our questionnaire, with its specific and indirect questions, training the interviewers to use specifying questions, has minimized the danger to a great extent but has not eliminated it completely. The remedy lies in the direction of still more specific and concrete questions.

INDEX

Adams family, 29-33, 45, 48, 115
Age, distribution of among family members, 135
Authority: classification of authority relations, 50-53; criteria of types of, 146-153; defined, 9; ground of, defined, 10; loss of, defined, 10-15. *See also* Father's authority

Baldwin family, 38, 72, 120-121
Birth control, *see* Sex relations
Brady family, 46-47, 97-101
Brown family, 67

Cavan, Ruth Shonle, 15
Church: as compensation for loss of status, 98 f.; decline in attendance of, 125; religious affiliations of the families and, 134
Class attitudes: effect of unemployment upon, 117-122; lack of solidarity with others on relief, 128; prior to unemployment, 116 f.
Clubs, decline in membership, 125
Cutter family, 194-196

Decisive features: defined, 36-37; in breakdown of father's status, 92-102; of husband's status, 37-42
Discerning: defined, 22; described, 135-146
Dorrance family, 46, 101

Father's authority: and age of child, 86-89; and child rearing, 84-86; decisive features in breakdown of, 92-103; frequency of breakdown of, by sex of child, 86; and working son, 97-101
Fucini family, 39, 44, 133

Garland family, 38, 49, 132-133
Gessell family, 122

Holman family, 34-36, 45
Horkheimer, Max, 3

Husband's authority: compared with father's authority in extent of breakdown, 88-89; decisive features in breakdown of, 36-42; frequency of breakdown of, 23-24; patterns of breakdown of, illustrated, 24-36; reaction of husband to breakdown of, 42-48; relative strength of, prior to unemployment, 58-59, 70; voluntary relinquishment of, 12-14, 41-42. *See also* Marriage; Patriarchal traditions
Husband's personality changes due to unemployment, 66-68, 74-83; and authority with wife, 40-42, 68-73

Interview: approach to families, 5-6; duplicate interviews, 21, 153-160; techniques of, 15-21

Johnson family, 7-9

Kilpatrick family, 64-65, 72

Lake family, 1, 67
Leading questions, 21
Leisure: and relations with wife, 39-40; loss of daily work routine and, 81-82; with children, 90-92. *See also* Church; Clubs; Social life

Marriage: criteria of dominance in, 150-153; criteria of wife's attitudes in, 146-150; kinds of relations in, and fate of husband's authority, 54-65, 69-73; preunemployment relations in, classified, 50-53. *See also* Patriarchal traditions
Meyer family, 49
Mother: attitude of, and fate of father's authority, 114-115; role in child rearing, 84-86

Nativity of the families, 134

161

Occupations of the men prior to unemployment, 134
Olsen family, 56

Page family, 61-62, 78-81, 125
Patriarchal traditions: and marriage, 59-62, 74-78; and parental relations, 111-112
Patterson family, 25-29, 38
Pecuniary values and reaction to depression, 78-81, 126-127
Political views of unemployed men, 116-122; and radicalism, 120-122

Relief: children's attitude toward, 126-127; duration of, 134. *See also* Class attitudes

Robinson family, 93-94, 101
Roland family, 44

Scott family, 40-41, 79-81
Selection of families for study, 4, 134-135
Sex relations, effect of unemployment on, 130-133
Smith family, 62-64
Social life: of adults, 122-126; of children, 126-128
Status, *see* Authority

Tice family, 47

Wallace family, 41-42
Wilson family, 1-62

SELECTED BIBLIOGRAPHY

Angell, R. C. *The Family Encounters the Depression.* Scribner, 1936.

Brierly, W. *Means Test Man.* London, Methuen, 1935.

Cavan, Ruth Shonle, and Ranck, Katherine Howland. *The Family and the Depression: A Study of 100 Chicago Families.* University of Chicago Press, 1938.

Clague, E. C., and Bakke, W. W. *After the Shutdown.* Yale University Press, 1934.

Federal Writers Project of W.P.A. *These Are Our Lives.* University of North Carolina Press, 1939.

Gellhorn, Martha E. *The Trouble I've Seen.* Morrow, 1936.

Horkheimer, M., editor. *Studien über Autorität und Familie, "Forschungsgerichte aus dem Institut für Sozialforschung."* Paris, Félix Alcan, 1936.

Lynd, R. S., and H. M. *Middletown in Transition.* Harcourt Brace, 1937.

Morgan, Winona L. *The Family Meets the Depression.* University of Minnesota Press, 1939.

Stouffer, Samuel A., and Lazarsfeld, Paul F. *Research Memorandum on the Family in the Depression.* New York, Social Science Research Council, 1937.

Zimmerman, Carle C., and Whetten, Nathan L. *Rural Families on Relief.* U. S. Government Printing Office, Washington, 1939.